The American Assembly, *Columbia University*

ETHNIC RELATIONS
IN AMERICA

Prentice-Hall, Inc., *Englewood Cliffs, New Jersey*
A SPECTRUM BOOK

Library of Congress Cataloging in Publication Data
Main entry under title:

ETHNIC RELATIONS IN AMERICA.

Background papers for the sixty-first
American Assembly held at Arden House, Harriman,
New York, from November 12 to 15, 1981.
"A Spectrum Book."
Includes index.
Contents: Ethnic groups in American history / Stephan Thernstrom—Immigration and the American future / Charles B. Keely—The impact of ethnicity upon urban America / Robert C. Weaver—[etc.]
   1. Minorities—United States—Congresses.
2. United States—Ethnic relations—Congresses.
I. Liebman, Lance. II. American Assembly.
E184.A1E84   305.8′00973   82-552
                                   AACR2

ISBN 0-13-291682-7

ISBN 0-13-291674-6 {PBK.}

Editorial/production supervision by Betty Neville
Manufacturing buyer: Barbara A. Frick
Cover design by Jeannette Jacobs

10 9 8 7 6 5 4 3 2 1

This Spectrum Book can be made available to businesses and organizations at a special discount when ordered in large quantities. For more information, contact:

Prentice-Hall, Inc.
General Publishing Division
Special Sales
Englewood Cliffs, New Jersey 07632

PRENTICE-HALL INTERNATIONAL, INC. *(London)*
PRENTICE-HALL OF AUSTRALIA PTY. LIMITED *(Sydney)*
PRENTICE-HALL OF CANADA, LTD. *(Toronto)*
PRENTICE-HALL OF INDIA PRIVATE LIMITED *(New Delhi)*
PRENTICE-HALL OF JAPAN, INC. *(Tokyo)*
PRENTICE-HALL OF SOUTHEAST ASIA PTE. LTD. *(Singapore)*
WHITEHALL BOOKS LIMITED *(Wellington, New Zealand)*

Table of Contents

Preface

As a nation composed very largely of immigrant groups from various parts of the world, the United States has long been aware of the rich ethnic diversity which colors our national character. However, during the past twenty years, increased emphasis has been placed upon ethnic identity by those who have discovered a new pride in their ancestral roots and have chosen to celebrate the cultural and linguistic traditions which are their heritage.

With this change in our society have also come changes in our laws, regulations, and practices to reflect the different perceptions of our nation as an amalgam of groups rather than purely a collection of families and individuals. These changes, especially those reflecting controversial court cases, have introduced new frictions into the relationships among ethnic groups in the United States.

In order to seek ways to ease tensions among groups and to find a basis for constructive dialogue among them, especially in large metropolitan areas, The American Assembly convened a meeting among government officials, leaders of ethnic communities, businessmen and women, academicians, jurists, and representatives of the communications media at Arden House, Harriman, New York, from November 12 to 15, 1981. In preparation for that meeting, The Assembly retained Professor Lance Liebman of Harvard Law School as editor of the undertaking. Under his editorial supervision, background papers on various aspects of ethnic group relations were prepared and read by the participants in the Arden House discussions.

Those background papers have been compiled into the present volume, which is published as a stimulus to further thinking and discussion about this subject among informed and concerned citizens. We hope this book will serve to provoke a broader national consensus for policies designed to improve relations among ethnic groups.

Funding for this project was provided by the Ford Foundation, the Carnegie Corporation, the New York Times Foundation, GEICO, and Mrs. Kathleen H. Mortimer. The opinions expressed in this volume are those of the individual authors and not necessarily those of the sponsors nor of The American Assembly, which does not take stands on the issues it presents for public discussion.

William H. Sullivan
President
The American Assembly

Acknowledgments

Acknowledgment is gratefully made to the following for permission to reprint excerpts from works published by them:

Felicia Lamport for the excerpt from her poem "Minorities Priorities" from Felicia Lamport, *A Book for Boston*. It appears on page 1.

Atheneum Publishers, Inc., for the excerpt on page 80 from Stephen Steinberg, *The Ethnic Myth: Race, Ethnicity, and Class in America* (New York: Atheneum, 1981). Copyright © 1981 by Stephen Steinberg. Reprinted with the permission of the publisher.

MIT Press for the excerpts on pages 128 and 139 from Nathan Glazer and Daniel P. Moynihan, *Beyond the Melting Pot*. Used by permission of the publisher.

The *New York Times* for the excerpt that appears on page 141 from "The Week of the Unelection," September 12, 1981. Copyright © 1981 by The New York Times Company. Reprinted by permission.

Lance Liebman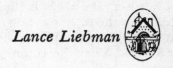

Introduction

Much is new in America's domestic politics today. Many aspects of the New Deal settlement, carried to or beyond fullness in the 1960s, are now in the process of being reconsidered. Issues that seemed closed are now open. Yet with all the new talk and new action, much remains the same, especially in our large cities. Youth unemployment, fiscal pressure, ineffective schools, illegal immigration, ethnic rivalry: these are facts of the eighties as they were of the sixties and seventies, and the policy alternatives seem neither new nor especially hopeful.

When so much is new, yet so much is the same, the challenge for thoughtful actors and for active thinkers is acute. This is a time when it is essential to see situations clearly, a time to ask honestly what we have learned and what that we thought true is false, and a time to consider new policies and reconsider old ones with as much freedom from sentiment and ideology and self-interest as we can possibly achieve.

This volume attempts clear thought and honest exchange of views about the interconnected issues that have been clumsily called "Ethnic Relations." The scope is very broad. We are concerned with the different people who live in the United States, with immigration and language and schools and neighborhoods

LANCE LIEBMAN _is associate dean and professor of law at Harvard University. Previously Professor Liebman was clerk to Supreme Court Justice Byron White and assistant to Mayor John Lindsay of New York City. His books include_ Property and Law, Race and Schooling in the City, _and_ Public Duties: Moral Obligations of Government Officials.

and jobs. On all these subjects and many more, government has had policies and programs. We need to know what has worked, what has not, and what is the right thing to do now. But, much more, we want to know how to think about the subject whole, what core values should be the starting point for thinking about policies, and what the country is in fact like and what we want it to be.

Diverse experts, asked to write on subjects that are pieces of the whole, have achieved a degree of agreement and coherence that is a pleasant surprise to me. If the authors who follow are typical of the breadth of thought in the country, then we do in fact have a range of agreement that may be much more significant than the differences which that agreement isolates and emphasizes.

This volume is intended to help its readers and the general American public focus on:

1. the realities of immigration circumstances, the choices we face in making and implementing immigration policy, and the relationship between immigration facts and domestic social circumstances;
2. whether we are becoming a multilingual nation, what our attitude should be toward such a development, and the impact of current and possible language policies;
3. urban political and social life, including policies of education, jobs, and public services, and their relationship to outcomes of assimilation, group consciousness, and group relations; and
4. institutional questions, including who should decide what issues; in particular, are the courts playing an appropriate role in America's political and social life?

All of us who have worked on these chapters believe that their subject matter is worthy of broad discussion as a path toward national agreement about difficult and divisive policy choices.

Stephan Thernstrom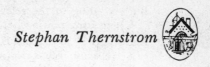

1

Ethnic Groups in American History

In the 1960s and 1970s the United States experienced a cultural earthquake. Or so it seemed from reading the press or watching the tube. The "unmeltable ethnics" were on the rise, and the WASPs—revealingly, the only remaining ethnic slur permissible in enlightened circles—were on the run. *E Pluribus Unum* seemed to be giving way to *E Pluribus Plura*. One black intellectual announced flatly that

> there *never* was a melting pot; there is not *now* a melting pot; there never will *be* a melting pot; and if there ever was, it would be such a tasteless soup that we would have to go back and start all over!

At congressional hearings on the bilingual education act, a congressman from New York announced that "we have discarded the philosophy of the melting pot. We have a new concept of the value of enhancing, fortifying, and protecting differences, the very differences that make our country such a great country." A light poem about Boston called "Minority Priority" summed up what was becoming the new conventional wisdom:

STEPHAN THERNSTROM *is the Winthrop Professor of History at Harvard University and director of the Charles Warren Center for Studies in American History. Dr. Thernstrom has received numerous fellowships, grants, and scholarly awards for his work in several areas, including historical urban life, poverty, and ethnicity in the American experience. He recently edited the Harvard Encyclopedia of American Ethnic Groups.*

Boston's very proud of its minorities,
    Delighted to be polyglot,
But according to the relevant authorities,
    A melting pot is what it's not.

Italian, Irish, Slavic, and Hebraic now
    Are sedulously sticking to their own,
Which makes the Boston picture a mosaic now,
    With every group as solid as a stone.

The reason is the hard and fast conviction felt
    By the members of each ethnic group
That as soon as a minority begins to melt,
    It's bound to wind up in the soup.

The editor of this volume has asked me to provide a "historical overview" that might help to explain why this happened. Why, he asked, does "the paradigm of the melting pot" no longer have "relevance" for "an increasing number of Americans?" Why has "ethnic identity assumed a significant place in the perceptions of citizenship?" I hope it will not seem churlish of me if I quarrel with—or at least significantly modify—the terms of my assignment. My interest is less in explaining the ethnic revival than in assessing the accuracy of the image of American society projected by its spokesmen. That is because I am frankly skeptical that there has, as yet, been much of an ethnic revival at the grass roots. The vast majority of American whites of European origin, I suspect, were entirely unaffected by it. (Nonwhites are another matter, a point considered at length later.) And for most who were affected it was a superficial and probably transitory experience. People who were "into" a search for their roots one year went into jogging, macrobiotic diets, or something else equally trendy the next. I suspect, in short, that Gunnar Myrdal, that well-known student of American race relations, was correct to dismiss the ethnic revival as "upper-class intellectual romanticism," and that before long we will see confirmed sociologist Herbert Gans's prediction that in a few years it would appear no more enduring than the much ballyhooed "religious revival" of the age of Eisenhower.

Pretty harmless, it might seem. So it perhaps was for the individuals involved. However, the ethnic revival was significant—and I think dangerous—at another level. The image of American society projected by its spokesmen gained surprisingly wide currency. American history became a story of ethnic oppression and

American society a mosaic of groups as solid as stone, with no cement to hold it together. Assimilation was denied, downplayed, or deplored; "Americanization" was treated as something akin to genocide. Groups who succumbed to it ended up "in the soup." I will seek first to establish that this is a highly distorted view of the historical experience of the tens of millions of European whites who crossed the ocean to America, and their descendants. Then I will turn to the complex problem of how blacks and various other American racial minorities have been faring recently. I will suggest that channels of opportunity like those open to earlier immigrants have at long last opened for them as well, but that the separatist strategies of advancement recommended by the new pluralists are likely to be ineffectual and probably counter-productive.

The Era of the "Old" Immigrants

By the time of the first census of the United States in 1790, America had already become an ethnically diverse society. The political and legal institutions of the new nation bore a strong English stamp, but people of English origins were actually a slight minority. Enslaved Africans and their American-born descendants made up 20 percent of the population, and there were large clusters of Scotch-Irish, Scottish, German, and Dutch settlers and smaller numbers of Swedes, Finns, Huguenots, and Sephardic Jews.

Over the next century and a third, ending with the restrictive immigration quotas imposed by Congress in the wake of World War I, the largest intercontinental migration wave in history deposited approximately 40 million people on American shores, a number *ten times* the U.S. population in 1790! Whether or not the American frontier was the great "safety valve" historian Frederick Jackson Turner thought it was, it is clear that in the larger context of Western history America was nineteenth century Europe's safety valve. Late in the eighteenth century, for reasons still not fully understood, a population explosion began in the British Isles and then spread into northern, eastern, and southern Europe. Population soared while an agricultural revolution was displacing peasants from the land before indigenous industrial development could provide work for them. America's inexhaustible stock of free land, and soon its burgeoning cities, offered them an alternative to mass starvation.

America also offered something more—remarkably easy access to citizenship and all the privileges it entailed, including a broader franchise and a government more responsive to popular pressures than any in the world. In the two centuries before independence the colonies had been hungry to recruit new settlers and provided easy naturalization terms, among other benefits, to attract them. That receptiveness continued through the founding years of the Republic. The Constitution drafted at Philadelphia gave Congress the power to "establish a uniform rule of naturalization," and the first Congress chose to confer citizenship after a mere two-year period of residence. The period was extended to five years in 1795, raised briefly to fourteen in the midst of the hysteria that produced the alien and sedition acts, and then restored to five years, where it has remained ever since. It should also be noted that many states, by far the most active unit of government in the early Republic, were even more liberal in their treatment of aliens and allowed them to vote as soon as they stepped off the boat.

Immigration law—rather, the absence of immigration law— reflected a similar confidence in the country's capacity to absorb strangers. The federal government did not even begin to *count* new arrivals until thirty years after George Washington's inauguration, and it was almost a century before it made any effort to screen newcomers. Like virtually every foreign traveller who visited the United States, Alexis de Tocqueville marvelled that "a society which comprises all the nations of the world, people differing from one another in language, in beliefs, in opinions" was nonetheless "welded into one people." The explanation was that American identity was not conceived in tribal terms, as a matter of blood; it was a matter of ideological conviction. Anyone who subscribed to republican principles of liberty, equality, and government by consent and who renounced allegiance to all other powers could become an equal member of the national community. (Any free white, that is. Barriers to the naturalization of various nonwhite groups would not be lifted until much later.)

PROTESTANTS VERSUS CATHOLICS

Of course there were limitations to the willingness of Americans to tolerate people radically different from them in language, beliefs, and opinions. The absence of restraints upon immigration and free access to political power after only a brief probationary period invited ethnic conflict. Tocqueville's observations were made when the ratio of newly arriving immigrants to the native population was much lower than it soon would be and when most newcomers were British Protestants. When people who were culturally much more distinct from their hosts began to arrive in much larger numbers shortly after the publication of his *Democracy in America*, ethnic tensions mounted. Two great spasms of nativist backlash erupted in the middle of the nineteenth century and again at its end. The first subsided quickly and had little enduring effect. The second gained enough momentum to achieve its objective of imposing strict and discriminatory immigration quotas that remained on the books until the Immigration Act of 1965. Before examining these ugly outbursts in more detail, I would stress that what is remarkable is not the frequency and intensity of conflict between natives and newcomers in American history, but rather the opposite. Given the magnitude of the immigration invasion and the cultural gulf between many incoming groups and the host population, the astonishing thing is that the United States was able to weld them into "one people" with so little fuss.

When clashes did occur, furthermore, they should not be seen simplistically as the result of WASP "bigotry" and "ethnocentrism." I have no brief for the Know-Nothing party or the Immigration Restriction League. But both were responses to profoundly unsettling social changes. Putting their supporters down as bigots is no substitute for an understanding of what moved them to action. They were indeed deficient in the toleration and forebearance we all should prize, but they believed that values they cherished were menaced by alien newcomers.

The first major nativist movement of the nineteenth century gathered force in the 1840s and climaxed with the formation of a new political party—the American or "Know-Nothing" party—

in the 1850s. It won sudden stunning victories in a number of states, but collapsed just as quickly in the midst of the deepening sectional dispute over slavery. Know-Nothing rhetoric was fierce, but the party's demands were actually fairly moderate. It did not seek to close the door to new immigrants but to make it harder for them to grasp political power by extending the residence requirement for naturalization to twenty-one years. It also demanded that Catholics be barred from holding political office, to foil an ongoing Catholic conspiracy to subvert the Republic.

In hindsight it is easy to dismiss Know-Nothingism as a classic manifestation of "the paranoid style in American politics." In fact, it was an understandable response to the first mass immigration of Catholics into what had been an almost uniformly Protestant nation. The Puritans who first settled America viewed the Pope as the anti-Christ; it was precisely the remaining Catholic vestiges in the only partially reformed Church of England that they wanted "purified." Many of their descendants continued to see "the harlot of Rome" as the source of most of the world's evil. Their conviction that Catholics were innately hostile to republican principles eventually proved mistaken, but it was not wildly implausible at the time; the Roman Catholic Church under Pope Pius IX was a major supporter of reactionary European monarchs and a staunch foe of republican revolutionaries like Louis Kossuth, a hero to American democrats but a "red republican" to the church hierarchy.

It is not surprising that nativists thought that Catholics lacked the independent political judgment necessary to the citizen of a republic and voted the way their priests ordered them to. They did indeed vote as a bloc. And they voted in ways that frustrated Yankee reformers. The most important reform drive of the antebellum period was not abolitionism—a very far-out cause even in 1861—but the common school movement. Catholics opposed universal, compulsory, tax-supported education on the grounds that secular and religious education were inseparable and that public education was a thinly disguised Protestant education. Instead they demanded public funds to support their own parochial schools. It was not sheer anti-Catholic prejudice— though there was plenty of that—that led Yankee Protestants to resist that demand. They believed that backing Catholic schools with tax dollars would Balkanize society by weakening what they saw as a key institution for shaping a cohesive national identity. As the example of Quebec suggests, they may have been right. It is important to note too that they did not go so far as to attempt legally to impose their brand of education upon Catholic students by requiring that all children attend state schools taught in English. In the Russian and Austro-Hungarian empires, by contrast, ethnic minorities were denied the right to education in their native tongue and subjected to high pressure campaigns to Russify or Magyarize them. The American middle way was not to foster pluralism with public funds but to leave individuals free to develop alternatives to the public system.

On a host of other burning issues of the day, immigrant Catholics took a stance sharply opposed to that of Yankee reformers and often had the votes to frustrate their efforts. The temperance movement spread like wildfire from the age of Jackson to the 1850s. Irish and German Catholics failed to enlist in the cold water army and flocked to the polls to defeat proposals to restrict or ban the sale of alcoholic beverages. And for Yankees involved in abolitionism or other antislavery activities, Catholics —especially the Irish—displayed antiblack and prosouthern sentiments that were deeply repellent. The sudden surge of Catholic power and the solid opposition of the newcomers to the most cherished Yankee reform causes lay behind the short-lived and unsuccessful Know-Nothing attempt to change the rules of the political game. It is striking that it was such a failure. Anti-Catholic sentiment would linger on for a century and more in some quarters and could be activated with powerful results on such occasions as the 1928 presidential election. But by the time of the Civil War, Catholics were integrated into the body politic to a degree that could never be reversed.

THE PROCESS OF ASSIMILATION

The cultural battles that preceded the war left an enduring imprint upon the political system. For generations to come Irish and German Catholics would lean toward the Democratic party, "the party of personal liberty," and shy away from the Republicans, the party of Yankee reformers. Other "old" immigrant groups arriving before 1890—the Dutch, the Czechs, the French-

Canadians, and the various Scandinavian peoples—also showed distinctive partisan preferences, depending upon the closeness of their cultures to that of the evangelical Yankee Protestants who dominated the Republican party. Differences in national origin and religious affiliation, recent "ethnocultural" historians have shown, were more important than economic status in determining how Americans voted for much of the late nineteenth and early twentieth centuries.

If the old immigrants displayed a degree of political cohesion, though, they certainly were not "solid as a stone" in other respects. American society was not a "stew pot" made up of many indigestible lumps. I am impressed rather by the rapidity and thoroughness with which these groups assimilated and will argue that the melting pot really did happen. I am mindful of the fact that the term "melting pot," as historian Philip Gleason has demonstrated in two splendid essays, has been used in so many confused and contradictory ways as to be practically devoid of meaning; much the same can be said of the concept of "assimilation." When I assert that ethnic groups did indeed melt, I mean that over time they became more like the old stock native population by five criteria for which statistical evidence is readily available. Of course these measures are crude and imperfect, and they pertain to behavior rather than consciousness. I believe, though, that they tell us much about the complex processes at work.

Linguistic Assimilation—Although most non-English-speaking groups sought to preserve their native tongue in the new land, none succeeded to a significant degree over the generations. That most immigrants learned English in order to function in the larger society is not surprising; it was highly functional for them to do so. The revealing development came in the second generation, which normally learned English in school but spoke the native tongue with their parents at home. There were exceptions, especially in isolated rural ethnic communities, but in general the second generation chose not to transmit German, Swedish, or Dutch to their children when they began to raise a family. Much of the substance of the Old World culture was thus irrevocably lost.

Occupational Assimilation—A major source of ethnic solidarity was the tendency of most groups to cluster in a few select occupations and work alongside their fellow countrymen. The longer they remained in the United States, however, the greater the likelihood that they would break out of their entry-level jobs into ones that were better paid and that involved more contact with members of other groups. An even more pronounced occupational shift was made by their American-born children. Although there were differences in rates of upward mobility between groups due to their cultural characteristics and the level of economic opportunity in the communities in which they concentrated, every second generation group moved into positions that had higher status and were less segregated than those held by their fathers. With the succession of generations, the average earnings of each ethnic group rose to approximate or surpass the norm for old stock native-born Americans of native-born parentage. The resultant growth of class differentials *within* each group—between the lace curtain and shanty Irish, for example—undermined ethnic cohesiveness.

Educational Assimilation—Although revisionist historians of American education have expressed much skepticism of late about the public schools as a melting pot, there can be no question that over the generations the groups who used them received an education that made them more like the old stock population in both skills and values. The Catholic parochial system might have offered an alternative to assimilation, but in practice it does not seem to have done so. The parochial system was closely modeled upon the public system, partly because its architects felt compelled to make easy transfer between Catholic and public schools possible. Indeed, the parochial schools run by English speakers chosen by the Irish hierarchy seem to have exerted a powerful Americanizing influence on non-English Catholic groups.

Residential Dispersion—Legend has it that immigrants typically clustered together with others of their own kind in urban ghettos or in farming communities inhabited chiefly by their fellow countrymen. In fact strong ethnic concentrations did not develop in American cities until quite late in the nineteenth century, when improvements in urban transportation brought about a residential sorting out of city dwellers along both class and ethnic lines. At mid-century the Irish of Boston and the Germans of New York and St. Louis were quite widely dispersed residentially. And when reasonably coherent "little Germanies" and "Swedetowns" did emerge later they were not as insulated and homogeneous as is usually thought. Their inhabitants rubbed shoulders with members of many another group; indeed, one reason English was acquired so rapidly was that it was the logical lingua franca for an incredibly mixed population. While ethnic clusters remained an obvious part of the urban landscape for many decades, furthermore, residence in them was a transitional phase for most ethnics. Those whose rising incomes gave them the resources to move out along the "tenement trail" did so, generally into neighborhoods of a more mixed character. The typical immigrant who had been in America for fifteen years lived near fewer of his compatriots than at the time of his first arrival. And when they grew up, his children dispersed even more widely.

Intermarriage—The principal source by which ethnic identity is transmitted is the family, and the key to an ethnic strength—indeed to its survival—is the propensity of people born into it to marry one of their own kind and to pass on that identification to their children. It is hardly accidental that the plot of Israel Zangwill's 1909 play, *The Melting Pot*, the source of that much abused phrase, was the conflict between the ideal of romantic love and the parochial desire of parents for ethnic compatriots as in-laws. That primitive question, "would you want your daughter to marry one?," is at the heart of the ethnic phenomenon. In this respect, at least, ethnic pride is ultimately indistinguishable from ethnic chauvinism; maintenance of the group requires that outsiders be regarded as inferior mates. Of course it is possible for the offspring of mixed marriages to identify with each parent in different contexts, to feel Irish on some occasions and German on others. But the more complex the family tree the weaker the identification with any one branch of it is likely to be. The old immigrant groups tended to marry within their religious tradition in the vast majority of cases, but national lines blurred quite quickly. Roughly 80 to 90 percent of the members of the immigrant generation married someone from the same homeland, but a distinct lower proportion of their children, and an even lower proportion of their grandchildren did so. A core of activists strongly identified with the group and an array of institutions remained, but over time their constituencies were steadily eroded by the inexorable workings of the marital melting pot.

The "New" Immigrants and the Restrictionist Impulse

In the closing decades of the nineteenth century and the opening years of the twentieth century, immigration into the United States soared to unprecedented heights. Between 1820 and the Civil War, 5 million newcomers arrived. By comparison, 5.2 million came in the 1880s alone, 8.8 million from 1901 to 1910, and an average of a million a year from 1911 to the outbreak of World War I. Few of them were from the British Isles and northern Europe; these were the "new" immigrants from eastern and southern Europe, almost all of them Catholics or Jews. Their cultures and customs seemed much more exotic and alien to the ordinary American of the day than those of the old immigrants; many, for example, bore Slavic names that were tongue twisters for an English speaker. The fears and hostilities they provoked produced a nativist backlash that succeeded in reversing America's historic open immigration policy and imposing quotas to keep out groups branded as "inferior" and "unassimilable."

Since most of the recent literature on the drive for immigration restriction has been written by liberal historians hostile to its goals, it is useful to insist on a distinction between the broad aim of setting a ceiling on the total number of aliens allowed entry into the United States each year and the specific national origins quotas that were enacted into law after World War I. One need not have been a bigoted nativist to have believed that some barriers had to be erected against the unfettered flow of immigrants into the United States. By the Progressive era America was no longer an underpopulated country with an open frontier. The old laissez faire faith in the invariably beneficent workings of the free market was under attack by reformers who insisted on state intervention in the public interest. American manufacturers, after all, had long been protected from the vicissitudes of the international market by tariffs. It was not inappropriate for other Americans to seek similar protection from the vicissitudes of the international labor market. Organized labor—with a leadership made up almost exclusively of immigrants or their children—had good grounds for supporting reduced immigration; they were incensed at the frequent use of the newest immigrants as scabs to break strikes.

Although respectable arguments could be made for some form
of immigration restriction, the most powerful ones offered by the
people who led the drive to its successful culmination were not.
The heart of their case was the assertion that the secret of American greatness lay in the intrinsic superiority of its "Nordic"
population—the first Anglo-Saxon settlers and the old immigrants,
who supposedly blended smoothly into American life because they
were of the same "race." The new immigrants were another
breed altogether, members of lower races whose "immemorial
hereditary tendencies" rendered them incapable of contributing
anything positive to the nation. Indeed, they were a menace: if
they intermarried with the Nordic stock, declared a leading an-
thropologist from the American Museum of Natural History, the
result would be "many amazing racial hybrids and some ethnic
horrors that will be beyond the powers of future anthropologists
to unravel." But one thing was certain. In such a mix, Nordic
man's "light colored eyes, his fair skin and light colored hair, his
straight nose and his splendid fighting and moral qualities" would
be bound to disappear. By allowing the free entry of people "from
the lowest stratum of the Mediterranean basin and the Balkins,
together with the hordes of the wretched submerged populations
of the Polish ghettos," true Americans were committing "race
suicide."

These new racist views were promoted by the Boston Brahmins
who founded the Immigration Restriction League in 1894. They
could claim the support of the new science of genetics, which revealed the vital importance of heredity in plant and animal populations. After 1910, with the publication of a massive study of the
immigration population by the U.S. Immigration Commission,
they could point to a massive body of social scientific "evidence"
as well. The Immigration Commission, headed by Senator William Dillingham, began its work with the assumption that the
new immigrants were racially inferior to their predecessors. It
manipulated forty-two volumes of statistical data in an attempt
to establish that southern and eastern Europeans were an unassimilable lump in the body politic and a threat to the social order.
It was ridden with fallacies, the most egregious of them its failure
to raise the question of whether the superiority of old to new
immigrants on a host of measures was a simple function of their
longer residence in the country and consequently greater op-

portunity to climb the social ladder. Buried in the report was ample evidence that the new immigrants were not inferior to their predecessors when length of residence was controlled for, and an enormous body of subsequent literature has shown that southern and eastern Europeans assimilated as rapidly as earlier groups as measured by such indexes as language shift, occupational mobility, intermarriage rates, and the like. But it was the predetermined conclusions of the Dillingham report, not its hard evidence, that mattered politically. It was generally taken to be powerful social scientific proof of the need to bar the door to all but "Nordic" newcomers.

Although the core sentiment behind the restrictionist drive was racist, the first device proposed to check immigration was not overtly so. It was the literacy test. Supporters of the measure clearly assumed that most of the new immigrants would flunk, but they thought it politic to make the standard for admission a seemingly neutral one. A ban on illiterate immigrants passed Congress as early as 1896 but was vetoed by Grover Cleveland. Similar measures passed in 1913 and 1915, again to meet with presidential vetoes.

The xenophobia stirred up by three years of argument over the war in Europe gave the literacy test the final push it needed; Congress passed the bill over Wilson's veto on the eve of American entry into the conflict. The likelihood that the United States would be drawn in put impossible strains upon a society that had drawn a large fraction of its population from one of the countries now at war and stirred a frantic concern for "100 percent Americanism." Although Wilson opposed the literacy test, his charge that critics of his foreign policies had un-American "divided loyalties" provided ammunition for the Immigration Restriction League. Wilson denounced "hyphenates," who had hyphens in their names because they had come from Europe with their bodies but had left their hearts behind. Wilson claimed to be impartial in his attacks on hyphenism. "A man who thinks of himself as belonging to a particular national group in America," he said, "has not yet become an American." But he behaved as if only the new immigrants, plus older groups with grudges against Britain like the Germans and Irish, were hyphenates. Americans of British stock (like Wilson himself) were free to back Britain without being accused of giving their "soul-allegiance to some foreign power." In 1917 his ambassador to Britain, Walter Hines Page, displayed his own form of hyphenism while denouncing another: "We Americans have to throw away our provincial ignorance, hang our Irish agitators and shoot our hyphenates, and bring up our children with reverence for English history and in awe of English literature."

To be 100 percent American thus was to be Anglo-American. The result was a drastic narrowing of Israel Zangwill's original cosmopolitan vision of the melting pot, in which all of the diverse groups included in the American population mixed together to form a new and better species. The war promoted a preservationist mentality; only those newcomers who fitted into an already fixed national pattern would be welcomed. It was the conception behind the Americanization classes conducted at Henry Ford's huge Dearborn plant in the 1920s. A gigantic wooden pot was erected on the stage for the graduation ceremony. Graduates would march into it wearing Old World costumes, singing native folk songs. The teachers stood on the edge stirring the pot with big spoons. And then the door would open, and out marched the immigrants in American dress, singing the "Star-Spangled Banner." In the old version of the melting pot, the teachers would have been inside as well, being changed into something new. Now assimilation had become sheer Anglo-conformity. Perhaps the most amazing manifestation of this new parochialism was the fact that by 1919 no less than fifteen states had passed laws forbidding instruction in any foreign language in the public schools! Americans evidently had to be protected from corrupting contact with minds like Goethe, Dante, Cervantes, and Tolstoy.

The Red Scare reinforced popular fears that the new immigrants would never conform to American ways. Most of the targets of A. Mitchell Palmer's "Red Raids" were aliens from eastern or southern Europe. The old immigrants, said the secretary of labor, were "the beaver type that built up America"; the new immigrants were "rat-men trying to tear it down," bomb-throwing revolutionaries striking at "the foundations of society." Manufacturers, traditionally firm supporters of the free immigration that provided them with low-cost labor, swung to the other side out of fear of the alien radical. "We have enough immigrants from southern Europe to last us for the next fifty years if we are to maintain Americanism," said a coal company president.

The literacy test, it quickly became apparent, would not be enough to "maintain Americanism." It was completely ineffectual, in fact, because restrictionists had underestimated the literacy of Europeans seeking entry into the United States. In 1920, 500,000 immigrants passed the test and gained entry; in 1921 over 800,000 did, about as many as in a typical prewar year. Worse yet, the vast majority were from the despised new immigrant nationalities. Congress then moved to close the gates, decisively and with very little dissent. First, it set a firm limit on the total number of newcomers, however well-qualified, who would be admitted into the country. The 1921 quota act fixed the annual level at only 40 percent of the average that had prevailed before the war; a 1924 bill cut it to less than 20 percent.

Even more significant, Congress apportioned quotas for specific countries in a manner that was nakedly discriminatory. Newcomers were admitted not in proportion to the number who wished to immigrate or some other neutral standard. Instead, a formula was chosen that strongly favored applicants from northern and western Europe and eliminated almost entirely those from southern and eastern Europe, precisely the countries in which economic and demographic pressures had produced the largest pools of people eager to leave. The 1924 act specified that immigrants from a given country could be admitted in accord with the proportion of their fellow countrymen living in the United States in *1890*, before the mass immigration from southern and eastern Europe had begun. The quotas for the British, Scandinavians, and Germans turned out to be only slightly below the actual number of people who had chosen to come to the United States from those countries in the immediate prewar years, but the number of Italians, Poles, Greeks, and east European Jews allowed to enter was slashed to a mere 3 percent of the prewar average.

It is not quite true, as is often thought, that these drastic steps entirely "closed the golden door." There were many loopholes, the most important of which was that countries in the Western Hemisphere were exempted from the quotas. As a result, over half a million Mexicans and a million French- or British-Canadians entered the U.S. in the 1920s. Even after 1924 the United States had one of the most liberal immigration policies of any advanced industrial society, far more so than Britain or France, for example. Still, the restrictive immigration laws passed in the 1920s marked a major departure from the older American faith that all people were capable of flourishing in conditions of freedom. Although some exceptions were made for displaced persons and refugees after World War II, it was not until 1965 that the United States abandoned a quota system that ranked the "races" of the world in the order of their supposed desirability and assimilability and hence advised millions of Americans of new immigrant stock that a majority of their fellow countrymen regarded them as inferior material.

ASSIMILATION OF THE "NEW" IMMIGRANTS

By then—ironically on the very eve of the "discovery" that the melting pot had not really melted—it seemed plain to most Americans that it had. I suspect that the renewed confidence in America's capacity to absorb strangers that the liberalized immigration law attested to had much to do with the general conviction that the new immigrants had proven to be just as assimilable as the old immigrants. The great backlash stirred up by World War I remained strong through the twenties, as suggested by the dramatic rise of the second Ku Klux Klan and the fratricidal war within the Democratic party over the Klan and Prohibition. Ethnic tensions began to subside in the Great Depression and eased further during World War II and the remarkable economic boom that followed it.

Of course ethnic distinctions did not disappear altogether, even among the third generation (though they did not increase either, as "Hansen's law" would have it). The descendants of new immigrants—or for that matter those of old immigrant stock in many cases—were not randomly scattered across the American landscape and evenly dispersed throughout the social structure. Each group had some remaining residential and occupational clusters, some institutional life, some visible leadership, and a core of people who identified strongly with it. But over time the proportion of such people was clearly shrinking. Judged by the five assimilation indexes employed earlier, they displayed the same pattern as the old immigrants—rapid disappearance of non-English native tongues, occupational mobility, rising educational attainments, and declining endogamy. Only the last—but the most important—of these points needs illustration here. A study of a 1963 national sample of American Catholics measured trends in intermarriage rates for six European groups and found a decline in in-group marriages over the generations for every one. By the third generation over 50 percent of the members of each were choosing an outsider; with the Irish the proportion was over 75 percent.

Religious lines were slower to blur; most of their marriages were to other Catholics, as suggested by Will Herberg's "triple melting pot" theory in his book *Protestant, Catholic, Jew*. But the boundaries between religious groups were also becoming quite porous. The case of the Jews, so often mistakenly seen as a "model American ethnic minority," is particularly instructive. The Jews may be a "model" for their cultural achievements, but they have a number of characteristics that distinguish them from national origins groups like the Italians, Poles, or Hungarians. With an exclusive religion, a history of thousands of years of survival as a separate people in Diaspora, high levels of concentration in only a few of the largest metropolitan areas with long-settled Jewish communities, and the galvanizing experience of the Holocaust and the birth of Israel, Jews were in a better position to keep their children marrying within the flock than any European group. Until World War II they succeeded. Of the Jews marrying in New York City around 1910, only 1 percent took a non-Jewish partner, and subsequent studies down through the 1930s put the figure at 3 percent or less. By 1961–65, the rate of out-marriage had climbed to 17 percent, and for 1966–72 it was almost double that—32 percent. It is true that in at least a small proportion of these mixed marriages the non-Jewish partner converted to Judaism. And it is true that the children born to them may frequently elect to identify themselves with the Jewish community. But there can be little doubt that if this trend continues— and I am not aware of any signs that it has reversed or even slowed—it will threaten the survival of the Jewish ethnic group in the United States. For other groups without the special characteristics of the Jews, the process has already gone much further.

The ethnic revival of our time, then—to the extent to which it is a real phenomenon rather than media hype—is perhaps best seen as the last gasp of groups nearing extinction. Assimilation, in this reading, had proceeded so far that the prophets of the

ethnic revival feel secure enough in their Americanism to assert
that they want their differences noticed and tolerated as well. It
is hard to find many real differences, since the original Old World
cultures have been so thoroughly eroded away, and few third or
fourth generation ethnics are prepared to put in the very hard
work required to learn Estonian or Serbo-Croatian, let us say,
and to study the history of their ancestors. Instead, they settle
for what Herbert Gans has called "symbolic" or "expressive"
ethnic identity which makes few behavioral demands upon them.
I cannot elucidate this interesting hypothesis further here, but
would suggest that ethnic differentiation of this sort—wearing a
"Green Power" T-shirt, say—is not something with any very important social consequences. Being Irish in Boston today in this
respect bears no resemblance to being Irish in Boston in 1851.

Ethnicity in the Era of Entitlement

The ethnic revival associated with the black power, brown
power, red power, and yellow power movements seems to me a
quite different phenomenon. Although it displays some resem-
blances to earlier clashes in American political history, it presses
new ethnic claims upon the state. A very early and prescient
statement of what is new was made by Daniel P. Moynihan in the
1965 report *The Negro Family: The Case for National Action.*
Moynihan argued that America's egalitarian ideal was acquiring
"a profoundly significant new dimension." It was "increasingly
demanded," he observed, that "the distribution of success and
failure within one group be roughly comparable to that within
other groups." The unfortunate furor stirred up by the Moynihan
report has obscured the fact that it articulated and endorsed a
"fair share" conception of ethnic entitlement that has since become the liberal conventional wisdom. A characteristic expression
is to be found in a 1978 report of the U.S. Civil Rights Commission. "The effects of discrimination and disadvantage," it asserted, "continue to prevent some groups of people from enjoying
the opportunities and benefits available to most of their fellow
citizens." There could be "no more important goal in the nation
than achieving equality of opportunity and equity of reward
among all persons, regardless of their sex, racial, or ethnic characteristics." Although a distinction was drawn between "equality

of opportunity" and "equity of reward," the report throughout conflated the two. Whenever a "minority" ranked below the "majority" on some measure of socioeconomic status, the commission took it as evidence that the opportunity structure was flawed and that remedial action by the federal government was imperative. Every group had a claim to a fair share, and a fair share meant an equal share.

The ideal of statistical parity was first advanced by those who, like Moynihan, were dismayed by the economic problems that afflicted the black community. But it was easily extended to other groups. The Civil Rights Commission's 1978 *Social Indicators of Equality for Minorities and Women* identified seven "minorities" —American Indian/Alaskan Natives, blacks, Mexican-Americans, Puerto Ricans, Japanese-Americans, Chinese-Americans, and Filipino-Americans. The report compared their status with that of "whites not of Hispanic origin" on a wide variety of social indicators. Just why these were *the* minorities to be concerned about and why all other groups were consigned to the "majority" was not revealed in the text of the report. Although the rationale is uncertain, a hasty footnote allusion to "the minority racial composition" suggests one possibility. The commission apparently assumed that these groups did not belong to the white race and that their "continuing severe social and economic inequality" was hence a cause for special concern. That young Americans of Polish and French-Canadian background had below-average rates of college attendance and were overrepresented in unskilled jobs was not a problem in the commission's mind, presumably because they belonged to the white majority. If the same held true for Mexicans and Puerto Ricans, though, it was necessary to develop "programs intended to remedy such conditions."

Do these seven allegedly "racial" minorities truly face handicaps different in kind from those confronted earlier by members of ethnic groups based upon common geographical origin, language, religion, and the like? The most common argument for sharply distinguishing between racial and ethnic minorities is that racially distinctive groups are denied the opportunity to adapt to the new culture and assimilate into the mainstream that was open to white immigrants. You can change your mode of dress, your speech patterns, and your table manners, the argument goes, but you cannot change the color of your skin and pass freely in white society. Anatomy—or rather physiognomy—is destiny. This is plausible but too simplistic. Skin color may be a constant—though it can change over the generations with interracial mating —but perceptions of what it means have varied enormously in our history, at times with remarkable speed. Within the past generation, racial attitudes have altered more dramatically and more fundamentally than in any previous period of our history.

This can be seen most clearly by contemplating the position of Orientals in the United States. The mass migration of Chinese coolies to the West Coast in the middle of the nineteenth century and the arrival of a flood of Japanese toward its close provoked racist hysteria about the Yellow Peril, forcing Congress to bar the door to further Asian immigration long before the triumph of the broader restrictive effort. The Chinese and Japanese who remained were denied citizenship and the right to buy land, barred from many occupations, legally forbidden to marry whites, attacked by lynch mobs, and otherwise treated about as badly as blacks in the Jim Crow South. During World War II the Japanese suffered the uniquely horrible experience of mass detention behind barbed wire in desert camps for four years, losing property for which they later received only partial compensation. And what of the Orientals today? The question embarrasses the authors of *Social Indicators of Equality for Minorities and Women,* who seem to have arrived at their conclusion that "for every indicator here, minority men have a long way to go to reach equality with majority men" before examining the evidence. The plain fact is that by almost every measure of socioeconomic status the Japanese are far *ahead* of "whites of non-Hispanic origin," be it the proportion holding professional, managerial, and technical occupations; educational attainment; median family income; or housing conditions. The Chinese are also substantially ahead of presumably advantaged whites on many key measures and fall modestly behind on a few others only because of a recent influx of uneducated immigrants whose lack of skills leaves them little alternative but ill-paid work in restaurants and laundries operated by their ethnic compatriots. And Filipinos, though mostly quite recent arrivals, have been making striking advances too. In 1960, for example, they rated twenty-six points below majority whites on a standard measure of occupational prestige; by 1976 the gap had narrowed to six points, and the proportion of Filipinos aged twenty-five to twenty-nine who had completed four years of college was exactly that for majority whites (34 percent).

Orientals today are about as physically distinctive, as racially visible, as they were a century ago. (Not quite, actually; those who were born and grew up in the United States are taller than their parents and closer to the American average, but the basic point stands.) But fears of the Yellow Peril have at last vanished, so the perception of racial difference is no longer charged with powerful meaning. When discriminatory barriers toppled after World War II, the traditions of hard work, thrift, and hunger for education that the Chinese and Japanese had long displayed made their spectacular upward mobility possible. They made the transition from being a stigmatized racial minority to a rapidly assimilating ethnic group. In fact, their marital assimilation is now so rapid as to call into question how long the Chinese and Japanese will survive as a group. In 1972 almost 33 percent of young Chinese and 50 percent of young Japanese were marrying non-Orientals.

None of the other "nonwhite" groups singled out by the Civil Rights Commission has advanced to the socioeconomic level attained by the Chinese and Japanese, obviously. Mexicans, Puerto Ricans, Indians, and blacks are at the rear of the procession on every measure. But not primarily, I suggest, because the hostility of powerful non-Hispanic whites still holds them back. The growth of racial toleration in the United States in the past four decades, illustrated by waning anti-Oriental prejudice, has been a much broader phenomenon. There are still bigots around, but most American whites have abandoned their earlier conviction that these groups were biologically inferior. Mexicans and Puerto Ricans were never as strongly stigmatized as Orientals or blacks by such measures as levels of residential segregation and rates of intermarriage, and they certainly are not now. Currently 33 percent of all second-generation Puerto Rican women, and 44 percent of those who are high school graduates, marry non-Hispanic whites; the figures for Puerto Rican males are even higher and only moderately lower for Mexicans.

It is hard to believe that the average Japanese-American family earns 75 percent more than its Mexican-American counterpart and more than twice as much as the average Puerto Rican family because whites prefer Orientals to Hispanics. The explanation for these differences lies in the differing histories and cultural characteristics of the groups. Most Japanese in the labor market today are at least third generation. Most Mexicans and Puerto Ricans (especially the latter) are relatively uneducated and unskilled immigrants or their children. Perhaps because of the severe prejudice and discrimination they have encountered, both groups, furthermore, seem to have been more resistant to cultural assimilation than earlier immigrants from Europe. They return frequently to the homeland, cling to Spanish, display limited zeal for education, have much larger families than the American norm, and are slow to rise occupationally. (The closest parallel in earlier immigration history is with the French-Canadians of New England before World War II.) These cultural and demographic patterns, constantly reinforced by the continuing flow of new immigrants, are strongly associated with poverty, and they will have to change if these Hispanic groups are to prosper. There are some promising signs that they are at present. A widely cited study of 1970 census data that concluded that third generation Mexicans had lower incomes than those of the second generation in fact established nothing of the kind; when proper age controls are applied to the data the expected generational advance does show up. Current bilingual education programs regrettably may slow the advance of Hispanics if they diminish the likelihood of students becoming fluent in English, as some critics have charged.

We are left with the blacks and the Indians. I will dismiss the question of America's 170 Indian groups as too complex even to touch upon in a brief essay like this. As for Afro-Americans, I recognize that no group in American history has been treated as savagely and exploited as cruelly and can appreciate the current apprehensions of black leaders about what life will be like under the Reagan administration. Recent historical studies show that not only in the South but in various northern cities in the late nineteenth and early twentieth centuries blacks faced barriers that were far more constricting than those in the way of European immigrant groups. Black migrants arrived with cultural handicaps that were a legacy of slavery—illiteracy, indolence, and dependence. But their concentration in a few menial jobs was too extreme to be explained by those cultural characteristics alone. Blacks were a stigmatized race and were deprived of the opportunity to compete on an equal basis. Not only were they kept out of the marital melting pot, but the rare instances of inter-marriage did not have a melting effect because their offspring were still regarded as black. Before World War II, the history of black people in America was unique—uniquely painful.

What has happened in the past four decades? Judged by the acid test of assimilation—marriage outside the group—not much. The rate of interracial marriage in the United States doubled between 1963 and 1970, but that was a rise from only .6 percent to 1.2 percent. I have been unable to find data for the 1970s, but I suspect that it rose substantially, especially among the college educated. The softening of antiblack stereotypes held by whites and the tremendous rise in the number of black students attending predominantly white colleges and universities must have had this effect. Still, interracial marriages are far from common-place. More important, the "one drop rule," the historic assumption that any trace of black ancestry makes one black, still holds force. The white racist fears that gave rise to it have greatly diminished, but now it finds support within a black community anxious to assert its own cultural distinctiveness.

Assimilation through racial amalgamation, then, is not a prospect in the foreseeable future. In other respects, though, the progress made by Afro-Americans in our time has been extraordinary. Its magnitude has been obscured because so much attention of late has been given to the issue of short-term change—whether the gains made in the 1960s continued, slowed, halted, or were reversed in the 1970s. A case can be made for each view, depending upon the precise measures and the base years selected. Of greater significance is the larger historical pattern about which there can be no debate: since the end of the Great Depression the black community has experienced a revolutionary economic transformation. In 1940 almost 25 percent of Afro-Americans worked in agriculture, chiefly as impoverished tenants or wage laborers; today less than 3 percent do. Only one black person in seventeen had any kind of white collar job in the depression era; now it is more than one in three. The proportion of black pro-fessionals, technicians, and managers has quadrupled in the past third of a century, and the share working as foremen and crafts-men has tripled. Those who worry that the ratio of black to white median family income slipped from .62 to .59 between 1975 and 1976 would do well to recall that in 1940 it was .39.

The average black aged twenty-five to twenty-nine then had only 65 percent as much schooling as his white counterpart; by 1970 it was 97 percent; and shortly after that the black rate of college attendance reached the white level. There are still large racial gaps in income levels, unemployment rates, and the like, but they disappear when one controls for demographic differences between the two populations—differences in age structure, family size, proportion of female-headed households, and educational attainment, primarily. Those differences are most pronounced among older age groups and should continue to shrink in the future.

Many fear that these positive trends will be reversed under an administration dedicated to budget cutting and hostile to affirmative action. I am not sanguine about how poor people, black and white, will fare as a result of the "Reagan Revolution." But examination of the pattern of black advance over the past four decades convinces me of one thing. An end to affirmative action may not have the disastrous impact some have warned of, for the simple reason that the greatest strides blacks have made toward socioeconomic equality in recent times were made *before* the federal government set forth "goals and timetables" for racial hiring in 1971. Substantial advances, indeed, had been made even before *Brown vs. Board*. It would take another chapter as long as this one to develop the point in convincing detail, but I am convinced that in the years since the outbreak of World War II, relations between the races in the United States have altered profoundly. Pessimists who contend that the Second Reconstruction might be rolled back just as the first one was seem to me ill informed about these two radically dissimilar periods of American history.

It may be a long time, though, before blacks equal whites on every measure of status; it may indeed be never. Although I am a committed egalitarian, that does not fill me with despair. I share the Civil Rights Commission's desire for greater equality "among all persons, regardless of their sex, racial, or ethnic characteristics." Equality of *persons* and equality of *groups,* though, are two very different things. It would be possible for black median incomes to rise to precisely the white level without benefiting at all the millions of blacks now living below the poverty line. Income among whites is now very unevenly distributed, and it is even more so among the black population. If the income gains that bring the overall black median up to the white one are all made by blacks in the upper-income brackets, the poor will remain unaffected. Something of the sort, in fact, happened in the 1960s and 1970s, political scientist Martin Kilson has recently demonstrated. To achieve greater equality of persons we may need not affirmative action—which primarily benefits the more affluent and educated elements of minority groups—but measures that redistribute income toward the poor of all races. The prospects for a coalition between the black poor and the white poor that might bring that about hardly seem bright today, but the future may hold many surprises.

Charles B. Keely

2

Immigration
and the American Future

The motto of the United States, *E Pluribus Unum*, applied
to the formation of the union from the several states. Metaphor-
ically the motto has been applied to the formation of a nation
from the variety of immigrants and their descendants. National
unity with ethnic diversity has always been a source of tension
in American life.

The responses over the course of the history of the Republic
have been varied. John Jay wrote in the "Federalist Papers,
No. 2:" "Providence has been pleased to give this one connected
country to one united people—a people descended from the same
ancestors, speaking the same language, professing the same religion, attached to the same principles of government, very similar
in their manners and customs. . . ." The description was not true.
It overlooked the Germans, Dutch, and Swedes concentrated in
the northern colonies; it glossed over the religious variety among
Protestants, not to mention Catholic and Jewish concentrations;

CHARLES B. KEELY *is a research associate at the Center for Policy Studies at
the Population Council. Dr. Keely has written numerous articles and papers
in the areas of population, labor force impact of U.S. immigration, and on
temporary worker migration in the Middle East. He has coedited* Global
Trends in Migration: Theory and Research on International Population
Movement *and written* Global Refugee Policy.

it did not give even a passing nod to the black slave population or native American Indians. Nevertheless, the quotation nicely illustrates the ideal of an Anglo-Saxon, Protestant nation that underlies the emphasis on conformity by immigrants. Whether expressed as 100 percent Americanism, opposition to hyphenated Americans, or in "Love It or Leave It" bumper stickers, the conformity ideal has been a continuous response to the tension. The majority did not always demand total assimilation, a complete casting off of the old self. Ancestry could not be changed; religious tolerance increased over time. But language and civic culture (principles of government) have continuously been areas where conformity has been expected and demanded.

A second response put the emphasis on the contribution of various groups to building the American character and nation. Israel Zangwill's play of 1909, *The Melting Pot,* was anticipated by 1782 in J. Hector St. John Crèvecoeur's description of America in his *Letters from an American Farmer:* "Here individuals of all nations are melted into a new race of men, whose labours and posterity will one day cause great changes in the world." The melting pot image is vague. Is it a stew in which everything that is thrown into the pot willy-nilly emerges as part of the meal, or is the image more like a smelter where only the useful metal is retained in the new alloy and the dross is eliminated? The melting pot idea is valuable: it calls attention to the actual and potential contributions of people from many backgrounds, and it indicates a greater tolerance of diversity as a source of enrichment. But as ideology and as description, the melting pot idea is as incomplete as conformity.

Horace Kallen, in his 1915 articles in *The Nation,* later published as a book, made the argument that true Americanism lay not in destruction of minority cultures but in their conservation. Kallen's argument made little impact on the United States immigration debate at the time. His idea of pluralism took hold slowly. But pluralism assumed a set of values about government and a set of institutions for conducting public business that was in large part a descendant of English tradition, however made over in the course of American history. Pluralism has been the dominant ideology of the last quarter century.

The Problems of Pluralism

The very existence of this volume on group relations in America is indicative that the United States is reevaluating the tension between the *pluribus* and the *unum*. Larry Fuchs, executive director of the recent Select Commission on Immigration and Refugee Policy, has analyzed this process of reevaluation, and I am indebted to him for many of the ideas in this section.

The civil rights movement and policy changes in immigration law in 1965 have both contributed to the reevaluation. The main thrust of immigration reforms in the 1965 legislation was the abolition of the national origin quota system, the mechanism for reserving immigrant visas for the exclusive use of natives of certain countries, primarily in northern and western Europe. The impetus for immigration change had roots in long-standing opposition to quotas based on principle, on experience in refugee resettlement, and on such human problems as family separation. But even interest groups such as labor unions that supported both civil rights and immigration reform in the 1960s by and large treated them as separate issues.

The change in the ethnic origin of immigrants under the 1965 law (from European to Latin and Asian dominance), the phenomenon of illegal migration which has dominated the immigration debate in the 1970s, and the refugee flows from Cuba and Indochina have created a linkage between immigration and civil rights policies.

PLURALISM AND CIVIC CULTURE

Pluralism assumed civic culture: the beliefs, institutions, rituals, heroes, and symbols that provide the basis for a common nationality. Civic culture is at the public end of a continuum between private and public domains. It is not difficult to construct a list of the basic values presumed to be at the core of the civic culture, but it is more difficult to agree on which are really central. For present purposes I suggest three values are important: individual freedom, equality at least of opportunity, and pluralism itself. A basic theme of the founding of the Republic was freedom from unreasonable actions of government and the right of people to govern themselves. The value continues today in calls for minimalist approaches to government. Equality of opportunity as an ideal emphasizes the right of individuals to pursue their goals based on ability—a downplaying of privilege that, like the freedom value, focuses on the individual. Pluralism itself has been added to the pantheon since World War II. Freedom and equality have come to be seen not only as compatible with but as requiring tolerance, and even respect, for cultural and ethnic diversity.

The point is not how well these ideals have been or are put into practice. Nor am I trying to suggest that the interpretation of these basic values is itself unchanging. The addition of pluralism as a basic American value illustrates the potential for flexibility. There is long continuity in the ideals of freedom and equality of opportunity, however, and defenders of pluralism harken back to the historical facts of religious, racial, and national variety in culture and social structures to legitimate the recognition of pluralism as a basic ingredient of the American experiment. As American as apple pie and pizza, and about time we recognized it, goes this line of argument.

What has raised the issue of redefining pluralism, and is different from the past, is the role of government in promoting and maintaining not only individual freedoms, but its role regarding equality of opportunity—including the movement toward insuring equality by requiring certain measures of group achievement —and its role in fostering pluralism. A list of actions from support of ethnic heritage studies to bilingual education indicates an active government involvement in fostering pluralism. Programs for equality of opportunity from affirmative action to minority contractors' set-asides illustrate the new government activism and the controversial emphasis on equality of achievement. In both these cases, there is tension with individual freedoms, for no longer is the spotlight of law and programs focused on the individual, but groups seem to have acquired, and group membership seems to confer, quasi-property rights.

The abolition of national origins quotas could be accommodated as a long overdue end to government discrimination on the basis of nationality, an aspersion on the ethnic groups who helped build the country, and unfair treatment of U.S. citizens in terms of their ability to sponsor relatives simply because they

were from a particular ethnic group with higher or lower nationality quotas for immigrant visas. The problem of immigration
policy reform was not so much getting rid of quotas. The
problems were created by one result of the legislative change,
the new dominance of immigrants from Asian and Latin countries.
The first problem was that the new immigrants became eligible
for programs seeking to bolster equality of access as measured
by equality of achievement. If affirmative action is to right past
wrongs, why should a recent immigrant qualify? In addition,
many of the recent immigrants have been skilled and professional
people. Over 25 percent of the immigrants under the 1965 act
who gave an occupation on their visa application were in professional and technical occupations. On what basis can one justify
their being categorized as a disadvantaged minority solely because
of ethnic ancestry?

Second, the concentration of new immigrants from Asian and
Latin countries, which are also the areas of origin of the bulk of
illegal migrants and the preponderance of refugees, has raised the
issue of the absorptive capacity of the American society. Some
questioning of absorptive capacity is a long-established and pre-
dictable response to each new wave of immigrants. What is different from the past is that the very groups focused on by policies
to foster equality are augmented in considerable numbers by new
residents within an atmosphere of government-sponsored emphasis
on ethnicity. If benefits accrue to persons by virtue of group
membership—not to mention political power to the group leaders
and other "professional ethnics"—will this not retard the process
of assimilation to the civic culture?

The worst case scenario following from this view is a break-
down of civic culture itself, a loss of agreement on basic values,
and a contest of interests that cannot be accommodated within
the political system. This, I might add, is different from the case
of Quebec, often referred to as a model of what might happen.
The variety, dispersion, and lack of a territorial base of Hispanics
make the comparison with Quebec not a particularly useful
guide. Yet, the threat to system maintenance is also greater, since
the territorial base provides a basis of accommodation and problem management in Canada that is absent in the United States.

Before getting carried away with the momentum of rhetoric,
it might be good to step back for a moment. The basic question

being posed is: what is the glue that holds the *unum* together? This is a fair and reasonable question which must be asked whenever the meaning of pluralism is brought into question. Whenever a central element of civic culture is questioned—slavery in the nineteenth century, segregation beginning in the 1950s— the coherence of the system is tested. The nation is now being tested. One way of characterizing the test is to say that pluralism is being redefined. The redefinition affects concepts like freedom and equality. Its reverberations are felt in the law, in education, in housing—even in impact on the psyche of men and women concerned about what kind of people we want to be. The tracks of the civil rights movement and immigration policy join at this juncture.

How the issues of *pluribus* and *unum* will be decided during this round of the making of America is not clear. To ignore the importance of either is to tempt fate. It is against this background that I discuss the issues central to the immigration policy debate and the political and economic forces, domestic and international, that shape the immigrant flows to this nation.

The Recent History of the United States Immigration Policy

The United States has always been of two minds about new immigrants. On the one hand, the country has historically been a refuge, a place of new beginnings, accepting and even recruiting new settlers to build the nation and its economy. On the other hand, the theme of protectionism has found recurrent expression in apprehension over the capacity of the culture and the economy to absorb newcomers, in the desire to limit labor market competition and assure minimal health standards, and even in nativism and racist theories. The history of immigration policy is a dialectic of these two themes of acceptance and protection.

THE MC CARRAN-WALTER ACT OF 1952

The basic immigration code of the United States is the McCarran-Walter Act of 1952. The legislation came after four years of congressional study and was passed over President Truman's veto. The McCarran-Walter Act retained the national origins quota system introduced into law in the 1920s. Based on theories of racial superiority, the quota system of the 1920s was a mechanism for choosing immigrants by reserving immigrant visas for the exclusive use of persons born in particular countries, mainly in northern and western Europe. The goal was to retain the ethnic distribution of the United States. Asians were barred altogether.

The McCarran-Walter Act retained the quota system as the main selection criterion for new immigrants. The justification was no longer racist theories but presumptions about assimilability, that people from countries with historical and cultural ties to the United States could be more easily absorbed. Asiatic exclusion was dropped in the McCarran-Walter Act and small quotas, mostly 100 per year, were assigned to Asian countries. Persons of Asian ancestry, however, were treated differently from others. A person of Japanese ancestry from Brazil, for example, was counted against Japan's quota, but a Brazilian of Italian ancestry born in Brazil was treated as a Brazilian. Within each country's quota, visas were distributed according to a preference system (Table 1). For high quota countries such as England, Germany, and Ireland, the preference system was of little importance since their visa quotas were consistently undersubscribed. Low quota countries in southern and eastern Europe and in Asia had long backlogs of people waiting for a visa. On a number of occasions in the 1950s special legislation was passed to clear backlogs or admit refugees as immigrants in excess of visa allotments. An important feature of the quota legislation period was that quotas applied only to countries outside the Western Hemisphere. For this hemisphere there were no quotas, not even an overall ceiling. Potential immigrants had to meet health, safety, and self-sufficiency criteria, which permitted a good deal of administrative latitude in controlling the volume of Western Hemisphere immigration. Another important feature of the quota policy was the restriction of natives of colonies to 100 visas annually, counted as part of the mother country's quota. The impact of this fell mainly on Hong Kong and British colonies in the Caribbean.

After 1952, presidential platforms of both parties called for immigration reform. In his 1953 State of the Union Message Presi-

TABLE 1. PREFERENCE SYSTEMS OF THE IMMIGRATION AND NATIONALITY ACTS OF 1952 & 1965

1952 Act	1965 Act
1. *First Preference:* Highly skilled immigrants whose services are urgently needed in the United States, and the spouse and children of such immigrants. 50 percent plus any not required for second and third preferences.	1. *First Preference:* Unmarried sons and daughters of U.S. citizens. Not more than 20 percent.
2. *Second Preference:* Parents of citizens over the age of twenty-one, and unmarried sons and daughters of U.S. citizens. 30 percent plus any not required for first and third preferences.	2. *Second Preference:* Spouse and unmarried sons and daughters of an alien lawfully admitted for permanent residence. 20 percent plus any not required for first preference.
3. *Third Preference:* Spouse and unmarried sons and daughters of an alien lawfully admitted for permanent residence. 20 percent plus any not required for first or second preferences.	3. *Third Preference:* Members of the professions and scientists and artists of exceptional ability. Not more than 10 percent.
4. *Fourth Preference:* Brothers, sisters, and married sons and daughters of U.S. citizens, and any accompanying spouse and children. 50 percent of numbers not required for first three preferences.	4. *Fourth Preference:* Married sons and daughters of U.S. citizens. 10 percent plus any not required for first three preferences.
5. *Nonpreference:* Applicants not entitled to one of the above preferences. 50 percent of numbers not required for first three preferences, plus any not required for fourth.	5. *Fifth Preference:* Brothers and sisters of U.S. citizens.* 24 percent plus any not required for first three preferences.
	6. *Sixth Preference:* Skilled and unskilled workers in the occupations for which labor is in short supply in the U.S. Not more than 10 percent.
	7. *Seventh Preference:* Refugees to whom conditional entry or adjustment of status may be granted. Not more than 6 percent.
	8. *Nonpreference:* Any applicant not entitled to one of the above preferences. Any numbers not required for preference applicants.

Source: Department of State, Bureau of Security and Consular Affairs. Report of the Visa Office (Washington, D.C.: U.S. Government Printing Office, 1968), p. 68.

* Amended in 1976 to require U.S. citizens conferring benefit to be over twenty-one years of age.

dent Eisenhower echoed President Truman's message vetoing the
McCarran-Walter Act by calling for a revision of immigration
law, especially the quota system. Indeed, President Eisenhower
sent a special message on immigration reform or mentioned it in
his State of the Union Message to every Congress (83rd to 86th)
that sat during his two terms as President. President Kennedy
also made a major effort to reform immigration. The result of
hearings on the bill prepared by the Kennedy administration was
a much-altered set of immigration amendments signed into law
by President Johnson in 1965.

THE IMMIGRATION ACT OF 1965

The 1965 immigration act, actually a series of amendments to
the McCarran-Walter Act, marked the end of an era. The bill
mandated the phasing out of the national origins quota system
by 1968 and ended the Asian discrimination provisions. The bill
also contained a new preference system, outlined in Table 1.

The Immigration Act of 1965 also introduced two innovations:
a ceiling was put on visas for immigration from the Western
Hemisphere and all nonrelative and nonrefugee immigrants were
required to obtain a labor clearance certifying that American
workers were not available for their jobs and that the immigrants
would not lower prevailing wages or working conditions.

The basic policy as of July 1, 1968, specified that 120,000 visas
could be granted to persons born in the Western Hemisphere and
170,000 to persons born in all other countries. The 170,000 visas
for the Eastern Hemisphere were to be distributed according to
seven preferences (Table 1), but natives of no single country were
to receive more than 20,000 visas annually. (Visas for persons
born in colonies were increased to 200 per year.) Those who
received a worker preference (third or sixth preference) and nonpreference immigrants needed a labor certification before receiving a visa. For Western Hemisphere immigrants, on the other
hand, there was no preference system and no country limit of
20,000 visas; however, a labor certification was required for all
visa applicants except immediate family members of U.S. citizens
and permanent resident aliens. In 1976, the law was changed to
conform the Western Hemisphere provisions to the Eastern
Hemisphere selection system. The only difference in the parallel
but separate systems was that the overall ceiling on annual visa

allotments was kept at 120,000 for the Western Hemisphere and 170,000 for the rest of the world.

In October 1978, President Carter signed into law a world-wide ceiling bill. This bill combined the two ceilings into a single, world-wide ceiling of 290,000 visas to be distributed annually, with no change in the preference system and other procedures.

President Carter also signed the Refugee Act of 1980 into law. This act removed refugees as seventh preference and reduced the world-wide ceiling to 270,000. Under the refugee act a mechanism for presidential-congressional consultation was established. After the consultation the President is to announce before the beginning of the fiscal year the number and areas from which refugees will be admitted into the United States and the U.S. interests involved in such admissions. If an emergency arises in the fiscal year, the President, after consulting with Congress, can increase admissions. The "normal flow" was envisaged as 50,000 per year, the approximate numerical average since World War II. The results of the first two rounds of consultation were 230,000 for fiscal year 1980 and 217,000 for fiscal year 1981. The Refugee Act of 1980 also made provision for funding domestic resettlement and made a number of reorganizations in departmental responsibilities for refugee policy and resettlement programs.

Table 2 presents a synopsis of the 1952 McCarran-Walter Act —the basic immigration code—and additional amendments contained in the acts of 1965, 1976, 1978, and 1980. The effect of each of these steps in the development of a world-wide policy has been a trend toward a larger proportion of immigrants from southern Europe, Asia, and Latin America. These changes in law, and the even greater changes in regulations for implementing the law, have resulted in an extremely complicated application process. One result has been growing dissatisfaction with a system that, in substance and especially in operation, favors the educated and wealthy who can maneuver themselves or hire guides to take them through the bureaucratic jungle and into the United States.

ILLEGAL MIGRATION

In the early 1970s, it became apparent that illegal migration to the United States had been increasing. Congressional hearings were held on the topic between 1971 and 1973 resulting in five volumes of transcripts with over 1,600 pages. The Immigration

TABLE 2. MAJOR PROVISIONS OF RECENT U.S. IMMIGRATION ACTS

Provisions	1952	1965[3]	1976	1978	1980
Ceilings					
E.H.*	158,561	170,000	170,000	None	None
W.H.*	None	120,000	120,000	None	None
Total	158,561+	290,000	290,000	290,000	270,000
Country Quotas or Ceilings					
E.H.	Proportionate to 1920 U.S. Ethnic Composition	20,000	20,000	20,000	20,000
W.H.	None	None	20,000	20,000	20,000
Exempt from Quotas or Ceilings					
E.H.	Spouse and Children of Adult U.S. Citizens	Parents, Spouse, and Children of Adult U.S. Citizens	No Change	No Change	No Change
W.H.	No Ceiling	Parents, Spouse, and Children of Adult U.S. Citizens	No Change	No Change	No Change

Preference System [1]

E.H.	4 Preferences	7 Preferences	7 Preferences [4]	7 Preferences [4]	6 Preferences [5]
W.H.	None	None	7 Preferences [4]	7 Preferences [4]	6 Preferences [5]

Labor Certification

E.H.	By Complaint [2]	3rd, 6th, Nonpreference	No Change	No Change	No Change
W.H.	By Complaint [2]	All Except Immediate Family of Citizens and of Permanent Resident Aliens	3rd, 6th Nonpreferences	No Change	No Change

* E.H. = Eastern Hemisphere; W.H. = Western Hemisphere.

[1] See Table 1. The percentages apply to the country ceilings in the 1952 act, to hemisphere ceilings in 1965 and 1976, and the world-wide ceiling of 1978 and 1980.

[2] No prior certification prescribed in 1952 act. A complaint had to be lodged or an employer had to petition for twenty-five or more applicants before a Department of Labor review was initiated.

[3] Provisions listed refer to systems as of 1968, after elimination of quota system of 1952 act and imposition of Western Hemisphere ceiling.

[4] The 1976 act provided that if a country met the 20,000 ceiling in any year, for the next year the preference proportions would apply to the 20,000 ceiling rather than the hemispheric or world-wide ceilings. This was to ensure that lower-preference and nonpreference applicants do not get squeezed out because of demands in the higher preferences. This provision is invoked in only a few countries where third preference demand is especially high.

[5] Seventh preference dropped and 20,000 visas removed from ceiling.

39

and Naturalization Service (INS) estimated that there were about one million illegal immigrants in the United States. The Western Hemisphere ceiling and the labor certification requirement in the 1965 act made access to an immigrant visa difficult for many natives of this hemisphere. For Mexico, the avenue of temporary labor was closed when Congress failed to renew the agreement with Mexico for the temporary farm labor (*bracero*) program, which had been in operation since 1942. Domestic opposition from labor, church, and ethnic groups over the effects on domestic farm workers' wages, conditions, and efforts to organize, coupled with opposition to migrant labor conditions (described by the Edward R. Murrow television documentary as a harvest of shame) led to the nonrenewal. The coincidence of these policy changes on temporary workers and Western Hemisphere immigration criteria led to the increase in illegal migration. Most Mexicans "entered without inspection," and apprehension at the border rose dramatically. Between 1964 and 1970, apprehensions increased fourfold, from 87,000 to 345,000. The number of Mexican nationals apprehended increased sixfold, from 44,000 to 277,000 in the same period. By 1977, total apprehensions were over a million and the Mexican total was 955,000. Non-Mexicans generally enter with a legal temporary visa (e.g., student or visitor visa) and overstay or take unauthorized employment. Increases in nonimmigrant visa denials in certain countries, especially in the Caribbean basin, also increased.

There are four areas of controversy surrounding illegal migration: the numbers, the labor force impact, the impact on social services, and social and political impacts of maintaining an underclass largely outside the law.

Numbers—It was the volume of illegal migration which first attracted attention. The apparent lack of concern of INS, evidenced in the Congressional hearings of 1971 to 1973, was reversed. Leonard F. Chapman, the INS commissioner in the administration of Richard M. Nixon, raised a clarion call about the "rising tide" of illegal migration, the inability of INS to control it, and its negative impacts on the U.S. work force and social services. Commissioner Chapman gave estimates of 4 to 12 million in various speeches. A whole literature on estimating illegal migration developed. Besides more resources for INS (but how much depended on the size of the problem), Chapman called for employer sanctions, penalties for those who knowingly hire illegal migrants. A provision in immigration law, known as the "Texas Proviso," exempted employers from penalties for harboring an illegal entrant. The proviso was originally inserted to protect agricultural growers. Chapman maintained that jobs were the force drawing illegal migrants, and employer sanctions would demagnetize the workplace.

A 1980 report by statisticians of the Census Bureau reviewed sixteen efforts to estimate the number of illegal migrants. They concluded that as of 1978, the number was almost certainly less than 6 million and "cautiously speculated" that it was between 3.5 and 5 million.

The annual additions to the illegal resident stock present even greater estimation difficulties. The stock is quite fluid and changes seasonally. Although assertions have been made that the annual additions were on the order of 500,000 during the late 1970s, no empirical basis has been presented to justify the number.

Labor Force Impacts—Throughout the 1970s, commentators alluded to estimates of illegal migrants and the number of unemployed Americans. Labor economists do not take seriously the implication of one-to-one displacement, nor do they credit the simplistic assertion that undocumented workers only take jobs that Americans do not want. Illegal migrants probably do displace some American workers, but more importantly they probably hold down wages and conditions. The availability of illegal migrants and their effects on wages and conditions is a kind of self-fulfilling prophecy that makes jobs less attractive to native workers. But undocumented workers help to revitalize industries such as garments and expand others such as restaurants. The revitalization creates jobs or retains them for Americans in these industries and complementary ones such as trucking. What is unclear is how deeply illegal migrants have penetrated U.S. industry so that the economy is structurally dependent on them. European countries found themselves to be dependent when they tried to reduce the number of guestworkers during the recession following oil price rises in 1973–74. The "temporary" labor force was not disposable workers.

In the aggregate, the U.S. economy probably does not suffer

from illegal migration, even after accounting for displacement, wage impacts, and income transfers to U.S. workers in the form of unemployment compensation, food stamps, and other income transfers. The heart of the matter is the redistribution effects— who gains and who loses. Employers, consumers, and workers in revitalized industries employing illegals and workers in complementary industries may gain while legal residents who are displaced or whose wages and conditions are dampened—mostly disadvantaged minorities—bear the burden.

Social Services—Numerous studies have found that illegal migrants pay more into the "system" than they take out in social services. While there is controversy over the representativeness of the research samples and bias resulting from this, the findings are rather consistent over many groups in many places. Illegal migrants generally pay taxes—federal withholding and social security—and are low service users. In the late 1970s, studies showed more use of educational and medical services than earlier in the decade, indicating a maturing of the migrant stream, the reunion of families, and a decline in the proportion of young adults in the illegal population.

The issue goes beyond biased samples. It is a distributional issue. There is no "system" in the sense implied by a general cost benefit analysis. That illegal migrants pay social security taxes but receive few social security benefits is fine for the social security system but of little help to the Laredo school system and the Los Angeles county hospitals. How to finance local services, paid in large part by local taxes because of failure of federal immigration laws, is the point of contention. These local burdens are not equally shared by states and localities but are concentrated in the Southwest and some of the older immigrant receiving centers in the Northeast and North Central states, such as New York and Illinois.

An Underclass Outside the Law—The final issue is more nebulous than the others but is nonetheless real. What are the social and political costs of maintaining an underclass, generally outside the law? If the glue that holds together the *unum* is frontally assaulted by sustaining a group with little mobility for themselves and their children and open to exploitation, it is foolhardy to assume that the debt will not have to be repaid.

REFUGEES

The third development in immigration policy, in addition to the changes in immigration patterns resulting from the 1965 act and the illegal migration of the 1960s and 1970s, is refugee admissions to the United States and the problems of international response to the global refugee situation.

Hundreds of thousands of Indochinese have been admitted to the United States; over 600,000 Cuban refugees have been admitted since the rise of Castro; steady streams from Eastern Europe and the Soviet Union have been admitted; thousands seek asylum from Haiti and Central America.

The United States has been a haven for millions of refugees. After World War II, most of them were from Europe. The people of the United States have continued by and large to give generously of themselves to help resettle each succeeding wave. But the numbers, the variety, and the cultural differences have raised caution flags. In the United States, the cautions revolve around capacity to absorb and the criteria for judging when a person is truly a refugee for whom resettlement outside his own country or the country of first asylum is the necessary last resort to avoid human tragedy. Internationally, the issue is the capacity of the international response to refugees to meet the challenge, especially since so much of the resources goes for expensive overseas resettlement. Over 97 percent of the estimated world refugee population is from Third World countries and in Third World countries. Are the international mechanisms and strategies developed in a European context adequate to meet the challenge? Should the United States be a country of first asylum for refugees from this hemisphere, and does that mean refugee camps? Can consistent criteria be developed to distinguish who is a "true" political refugee and who is an economic migrant, and can those criteria be evenhandedly applied? These questions, with their obvious foreign relations implications, are also important domestically, as is clear from the group relations problems posed by Indochinese, Cuban, Haitian, and East European refugees and applicants for asylum.

A Situation Out of Control?—Legal immigration, illegal migration, and refugee flow all contribute to a perception that immigration policy is out of control. It is this perception—and the difficulty of so many of the individual policy issues, such as criteria for admission of immigrants, policing the borders, employer sanctions, granting asylum, and the number of refugees accepted for resettlement—that fuels immigration debate. It should also be remembered that each of these issues and the perception of lack of control take place within the context of a period in which pluralism is being redefined. The controversies of the policy decisions feed into one another like a cybernetic system of inputs and feedbacks. As each of the immigration policy issues is described, it must be remembered that legal migration, illegal migration, refugees, group relations, and other domestic issues are all interacting to affect perceptions, the policy options that are even given consideration, and the policy choices that have been and will be made.

Major Immigration Issues

POPULATION DYNAMICS

The effects of immigration on U.S. population growth are the underlying issue surrounding debate on the numbers of immigrants. More narrow issues include whether there should be annual ceilings on immigration, how broad an amnesty for illegal aliens should be, whether and how quickly a backlog clearance should take place for the million persons now waiting for an immigrant visa.

POPULATION GROWTH

Legal immigration now accounts for 25 to 30 percent of annual population growth in the United States. With declining fertility, even a steady flow of immigrants will account for an even larger proportion of growth. When deaths exceed births in the United States—a situation already encountered in both Eastern and Western European countries—as a result of below replacement fertility, any growth, by definition, will be entirely due to net immigration. The increasing proportion of growth due to immigration is, therefore, a function of both declines in natural increase and immigration levels. Fertility levels are a more powerful determinant than immigration levels in population dynamics. Concern about the percentage of growth due to immigration can easily underplay this fact of American demographic dynamics.

Table 3 summarizes the effects of different levels of net migration, under different fertility levels, between 1980 and 2000.

The current total fertility rate (the average number of children per woman if all women had birth rates by age at the same levels as women in various age groups currently have children) is about 1.8 children per woman. Replacement fertility is about 2.11 (one child for each male and female plus a fraction—the .11 due to higher ratio of males to females at birth, infertility, and mortality to women before reaching childbearing ages). If current fertility rates continue—and assuming no immigration—the size of the population would eventually reach a peak and then begin to decline. Net immigration of about 800,000 plus current fertility levels would mean that the U.S. population would eventually peak and then remain at a level around 300 million. Immigration below 800,000 and current levels of fertility mean that the population would eventually peak—when and at what level depends on how many fewer than 800,000 net immigrants—and would eventually decline.

Table 3 gives the results of immigration from a level of zero to one million for three fertility levels: 1.8, 2.0, and 2.2 children per woman. More reasonable limits are net immigration between 250,000 and 1,000,000. That the U.S. would prohibit spouses from joining U.S. citizens, or that there would be no refugees, are hardly likely. But during the depression, the United States had a net outflow due to low immigration being exceeded by emigration back to home countries. On the other hand, the current concern over immigration (over 800,000 in 1980, legal immigrants plus whatever additions to the more or less permanent illegal stock minus emigration from the U.S. which is not inconsiderable even now) lead me to conclude that one million is an outside number as an average over the next twenty years.

It should first be noted that even in the space of twenty years, less than a generation, the impact of fertility is very great. At 250,000 net immigration, current fertility of about 1.8 versus total fertility 2.2 (a figure well below baby boom levels but still above replacement) means a difference of about 14 million. A policy eye must be kept on both immigration and changes in U.S. fertility behavior. Even at fertility of 2.2 and one million

TABLE 3. PROJECTED U.S. POPULATION SIZE IN 2000 AND GROWTH RATE,
1980–2000, BY LEVEL OF ANNUAL NET IMMIGRATION AND TOTAL
FERTILITY RATE

Total Fertility Rate	Total Population (1,000s)	Population Growth Percent Rate
(A) Annual Net Immigration=0		
1.8	243,677	0.3
2.0	250,348	0.4
2.2	257,722	0.5
(B) Annual Net Immigration=250,000		
1.8	249,539	0.4
2.0	256,318	0.5
2.2	263,809	0.6
(C) Annual Net Immigration=500,000		
1.8	255,402	0.5
2.0	262,287	0.6
2.2	269,896	0.8
(D) Annual Net Immigration=750,000		
1.8	261,265	0.6
2.0	268,257	0.7
2.2	275,983	0.9
(E) Annual Net Immigration=1,000,000		
1.8	267,127	0.7
2.0	274,226	0.8
2.2	282,070	1.0

Source: Adapted from Leon F. Bouvier, "The Impact of Immigration on U.S.
Population Size," *Population Trends and Public Policy,* Vol. 1 (Washington, D.C.:
Population Reference Bureau, 1981), p. 4.

immigrants, total population would be about 282 million at the
turn of the century. It is well to remember that because of concern that the population would exceed 300 million by 2000,
President Nixon appointed a Select Commission on Population
Growth and the American Future which made its report in 1972.
The focus of domestic concern for that commission was whether
Americans would adopt a two or three child family norm. Delayed marriage, delayed child bearing, lower family size, the rise
of contraception, and greater female labor force participation
are the various interacting trends that have led to the approximately 1.8 to 1.9 levels characteristic of fertility from the mid-

1970s. Although some demographers expect another baby boom (or boomlet compared to the high fertility levels of the 1950s), most do not see major reversals of the fertility dampening trends. Perhaps fertility levels have bottomed out and will go to higher levels around replacement levels eventually, but whether that will happen and especially the timing are uncertain. The sharp changes in fertility behavior between the baby boom of the 1950s and the baby bust of the 1970s naturally make social demographers leery about confident pronouncements by advocacy group oracles. Table 3 gives the parameters. My judgment is that the fertility levels of 1.8 and 2 and net immigration of 250,000 to 750,000 are the important entries. The range of U.S. population size and annual rates of growth in 2000 would be 250 million and a growth rate of .4 percent (1.8 total fertility and 250,000 net immigration) and 268 million and a growth rate of .7 percent (2 total fertility rate and a net immigration of 750,000). The current population of the United States is 226 million.

Immigration Ceilings—The total number of immigrant visas to be distributed annually is made up of three components: the 270,000 visas under the ceiling, visas for immediate relatives of U.S. citizens (exempt from the ceiling), and visas for refugees. In 1965, the major change related to numbers was to extend the ceiling to the Western Hemisphere. Adding parents to spouses and children as an exempt category and minor expansion (from about 155,000 to 170,000) of the Eastern Hemisphere ceiling to accommodate mainly the new refugee preference (seventh preference at 6 percent of 170,000 or 10,200 visas) were of secondary importance in the context of overall numbers. The need for a ceiling, even a partial ceiling exempting immediate family and refugees, is a virtually unchallenged policy position. But a "partial ceiling" seems to some to be a contradiction in terms and not an expression of tension over conflicting goals. In the whole post-1965 period, no serious exception was taken to reuniting immediate families of citizens. On the other hand, there was constant friction over the use of "parole power" to admit refugees in excess of the seventh preference ceiling. The parole power entitled the attorney general to admit persons for up to two years whose entry was in the interests of the United States. Originally envisaged as a mechanism to allow medical treatment or emergency care for accidents at sea, the power, often at congressional

urging, was used primarily for refugee admissions as in the case
of Hungarians, Cubans, Indochinese, and others. The 1980 refugee act prohibited use of the parole power for refugee admissions.
In all the cases where parole power was used for refugee admissions, Congress eventually had to authorize the adjustment of
those paroled to permanent immigrant. In the large-scale refugee
admission episodes, Congress realistically has no alternative but
to acquiesce to executive decisions. The 1980 refugee act was
meant in large part to resolve the conflict over use of parole
power.

The Select Commission on Immigration and Refugee Policy
in its 1981 report supported maintenance of the policy of ceilings
for immigrants with the exception of immediate relatives of
citizens and refugees. On the other hand, a bill, S. 776 (the
Immigration and National Security Act of 1981), was introduced
by Senator Walter Huddleston of Kentucky to place a limit of
350,000 on all immigration. The overall limit of 350,000 in S. 776
was down significantly from the earlier 650,000 limit in the last
Congress's Concurrent Resolution 24, also introduced by the
senator from Kentucky. The point was made by Senator Huddleston on an overall ceiling; the specific number is a negotiable
item.

The second issue about ceilings is whether to increase the current 270,000 visa ceiling for the nonrefugee and nonimmediate
family of citizens. The commission recommended an increase
to 350,000. The greatest disagreements were about the degree of
consanguinity for family preferences—especially brothers and sisters of U.S. citizens—and the degree of need for economically
related visa preferences, i.e., visa preferences for certain jobs, investors, etc. Proponents of expansion of any one category generally are politically forced to accept expansion of the ceiling
rather than a reduction of another preference group. Like the
use of many public goods, there is little incentive to reduce access
to visas by one interested party since others will not stop using
visas. The commission opted for expansion of the ceiling. The
legislative resolution of this issue is likely to be a function of the
contest over the criteria used to choose immigrant visa recipients.

Amnesty for Illegal Residents—Since the *Domestic Council
Task Force on Immigration Report* in 1976 at the end of the
administration of President Ford, successive government studies

have pointed to the futility, political cost, and inhumanity of massive roundup and deportation efforts reminiscent of "Operation Wetback" in the early 1950s. Thus, a legalization or amnesty has been proposed for undocumented aliens. The issue has been how broad an amnesty, usually translated into a cutoff date of entrance eligibility and a minimum period of residence. The Select Commission on Immigration and Refugee Policy recommended an amnesty with a January 1, 1980, entry date and suggested that Congress adopt some residency requirement but did not specify a number of years.

President Reagan's immigration proposals of 1981 recommended that persons in the country for ten years (five years for Cuban and Haitian entrants temporarily admitted by President Carter in 1980) be eligible for permanent status and that others be eligible for renewable three-year temporary worker visas and, when they have a total of ten years of residence, be eligible for permanent residence. During the ten years, the holders of the renewable visas would pay taxes but be ineligible to bring in relatives—even spouses and children—and entitled to no federal benefits (social security, unemployment insurance, welfare) except medicare, despite their payment of social security and income tax.

The amnesty issue revolves to a great extent around the number of people affected and the derivative demand for relatives in foreign countries to enter the United States to join their newly documented spouses and parents. Here we get into the morass of estimates not only of undocumented alien stock resident in the United States, but also of the further unknown—the distribution of that stock by year of entry which is needed to evaluate the numerical impact of various cutoff dates. Some opposed President Reagan's proposal as too stringent, unlikely to attract people to register (and, therefore, of questionable value), and a temporary worker program under another name. Others say any talk of amnesty is premature until illegal migration is brought under control by a strict enforcement program, and amnesty proposals will only attract more illegal entrants who hope for future amnesties.

Backlogs—The commission recommended allocating 100,000 extra visas per year for five years to clear up current visa backlogs due to oversubscription of preference categories or country ceilings. President Reagan's Task Force on Immigration made a similar recommendation, although the President's announcement of his proposals in 1981 was silent on the issue. The clearing of backlogs has been undertaken periodically since the 1950s. We seem continually torn between limiting immigration and seeking to clear backlogs when demand exceeds supply. To be sure, the interaction of country, preference, and overall ceilings under the 1965 act led to random patterns of backlogs and unintended anomalies, such as long waiting lists of spouses while some specialty cooks or live-in maids got visas right away. If the past is any guide, some relief will be forthcoming. Some wish to avoid repetition of the dilemma in the future by eliminating the preferences (especially the brother and sister preference) with the largest backlogs. The issues will probably be resolved by the contest over preferences that, together with demand patterns in response to the structure of the law, will dictate whether backlogs develop in the future that are so large that they are no longer temporary delays but virtual guarantees that visas will be unavailable for most on a backlog list.

Illegal Migration—Finally, it should be remembered that all these issues about population, visa ceilings, amnesty, and backlogs are influenced by the illegal migrant issue. One's assumptions about the current size and annual increase in the illegal resident population must color responses to various proposals on immigration. Illegal migration is the policy wild card that can vitiate any analysis of expected outcomes of a policy package.

SELECTION CRITERIA

Origins—The abolition of the national origins quota system in the 1965 legislation did not completely do away with nationality of immigrant applicants as a criterion for admission. The 1965 act set a ceiling of 20,000 visas for nonexempt immigrants for each independent country (and 200 for colonies—since increased to 600). This ceiling did not apply to visas for the immediate families of U.S. citizens. The reason for the ceiling was to prevent one or a few countries from dominating the allocation of visas under the preference system.

The operation of the 1965 amendment has led to sharp changes in country and continent of origin. Asia and Latin America (including the English-speaking Caribbean) have increased their share of total immigration. North America and northern and western Europe have declined, and southern and eastern Europe have held steady as proportions of total immigration.

The "composition" of immigration is almost a code word for national origins and especially the shift away from traditional European sources (including Canada) to increasing Asian and Latin American dominance. A variation on the composition theme is the concentration of Spanish-speaking immigrants. About 35 percent of 1968 to 1977 legal immigrants were Spanish speakers (and the proportion would be higher if net illegal migration were included). This concentration was higher than previous concentrations, e.g., 28 percent German speakers in 1901 to 1910.

The Select Commission on Immigration and Refugee Policy recommended maintenance of the exemption of immediate family of citizens from any ceiling, including the country ceiling. The commission further recommended that spouses of resident aliens and their children under eighteen years of age be included under the world-wide ceiling, but that they not be included under a country ceiling; rather, they should be taken on a first-come, first-serve basis to the maximum of preference for immediate family of permanent resident aliens. For all other preference groups the commission recommended a per country ceiling based on a fixed percentage of visas allocated to family preference (other than spouses and children of permanent resident aliens) and immigrants admitted under economic criteria, referred to in the commission report as independent immigrants. The commission included in these recommendations the proposal that colonies not be given a smaller ceiling (currently 600) under the mother country but be treated as independent countries, thus getting rid of that vestige of the quota system.

The commission justified the retention of country ceilings for the independent categories (nonfamily) by referring to the ceiling as a means to better meet the goals of independent migration. No hint was given as to why a per country limit would produce more desirable investors, persons of special merit, or those who could enhance economic growth. Similarly, the commission asserted that retention of the per country ceiling for family preferences (except spouses and children of permanent aliens who are currently second preference) "will facilitate the reunification of the closest family members without regard to nationality but still retain the advantages of per country ceilings in the other family reunification preferences." There was also no hint as to what those advantages are in the case of families, much less whether per country ceilings are the best means to obtain whatever the unspecified advantages might be.

It would seem that the last vestiges of the quota system are not gone even from high-level policy considerations. The commission report did not directly address the topic of the kinds of backlogs that may result from overall ceilings for family and independents, preference percentages, and two sets of per country ceilings that apply to some, but not all, family preferences and to independent category visa applicants. The issue of ethnic concentration of legal, illegal, and refugee migration and the impact on domestic group relations was obviously on the minds of commission members.

Labor Force Criteria—During the Carter administration there were calls for greater emphasis on labor force needs rather than family relations. The secretary of labor in the Carter administration, Ray Marshall, summed up the desire to upgrade labor force criteria: "Since most of the people who come to the United States work, we should relate the number of legal immigrants to realistic labor market needs." Proposals to implement this policy thrust have received little endorsement.

The Select Commission on Immigration and Refugee Policy generally opted for maintenance of the emphasis on family versus worker migration. The commission recommended splitting family and worker preferences. The new independent category (really a residual category for all nonfamily preferences) would contain visas for investors, for the extremely talented (world-class) persons, and for other workers. The commission favored specific labor market criteria for admission of these other workers but was divided over how strict the criteria should be. The disagreement seemed to be over labor certification. Some commissioners favored a job offer plus a streamlined labor certification (streamlined seems to mean the use of printed schedules rather than the individual screening of each application), while others favored retaining a labor certification process similar to the current one. There were suggestions in the commission report that 100,000 visas be available for the independent category. This is about 28 percent of the 350,000 versus 20 percent for current third and sixth preferences or a ratio of about 2.5:1 versus the current ratio of 4:1 family to job-related preference distribution. Some commissioners in the minority opinion statement said that the 2.5:1 ratio was a staff opinion and that the sentiment of the commissioners was to retain the 4:1 ratio of the 1965 act's preference system.

In short, the suggestion of downplaying family for labor force needs has not found enthusiastic support, judging by the lack of action and rhetoric in Congress and in the more active immigration forum of the commission. The commission did not move in the opposite direction, however, since attempts to dismantle the labor certification system did not prevail. Although the separation of labor from family criteria in the commission's recommendations is conceptually clearer, the recommendations do not herald a major departure in labor related criteria. The current drift is toward tinkering with the line-up of categories. The counteracting dissatisfactions with the relative emphasis on families; the lack of a policy to more closely align, if not integrate, immigration and labor policy; and the administration of the labor certification policy seem to be leading to the current impasse.

Kinship Criteria—The family reunion criteria have provoked some to say that the policy smacks of nepotism. The specific object of opposition is the fifth preference, brothers and sisters of U.S. citizens, because it is symbolic of the purported overreaching of family criteria and the possibility of a never-ending snowball effect of immigrants qualifying to petition for other relatives. The commission suggested retention of the fifth preference, President Reagan's Interagency Task Force suggested dropping it, and President Reagan's announcement of his proposals was silent on the issue. Within the commission, there was support to retain the brothers and sisters preference but only for the unmarried. This option received seven of the sixteen votes, while the recommendation adopted, retention of the fifth preference, garnered the majority nine votes. The battle is sure to be joined again in congressional action.

The commission also voted to expand the family criteria. The commissioners recommended including adult unmarried sons and daughters and grandparents of adult U.S. citizens in the exempt category. In the case of grandparents, no petitioning rights would accrue until the grandparent became a citizen, a provision to reduce snowball effects. Commissioners further recommended a numerically limited preference for the aged parents (ages sixty to seventy were discussed but no specific age was settled on) of adult permanent residents, if the aged parents had no children living outside the United States.

In short, the brothers and sisters preference is still in doubt. While this is the major point of contention, and the most significant numerically with almost a half-million backlog, an expansion of qualifying relationships was supported by the commission. These generally are justified on humanitarian grounds and include grandparents of adult citizens and aged parents (with no other children) of resident aliens. In both cases, the snowball effects are minimized or eliminated.

Grounds of Exclusion—The Select Commission on Immigration and Refugee Policy recommended that the current thirty-three grounds of exclusion not be retained. The content and phrasing were thought to be outdated and vague in many cases. The legal staff, with a large input by Commissioners Judge Cruz Reynoso of California, Congresswoman Elizabeth Holtzman, and Attorney General Benjamin Civiletti, revised the grounds to sixteen. While there was support for this revision, the major reason for not adopting it as a recommendation seemed to be fear of press coverage. Homosexuality, for example, was recommended to be dropped as a ground of exclusion, and the argument was raised that all the work of the commission would be overshadowed and perhaps disregarded because of headlines such as "Immigration Commission Supports Gay Rights." A number of commissioners specifically objected in their supplementary statements to the decision not to endorse specific revisions as a failure on the part of the commission.

In sum, the selection criteria issue often focuses on the weight given to the family and the labor force. The degree of kinship and the potential for snowballing visa eligibility have led to the charge of nepotism and to calls for rescinding the fifth preference. Even the recommendation by the commission to extend preferences was carefully drawn to avoid the snowball effect. The desire to use immigration to advance labor policy has found little support. The main emphasis of supporters of this view is to retain the goal of protection of U.S. labor. Tactically, this translates into retaining current labor certification procedures rather than allowing any dilution of them as a sign of weakening labor protection policy in immigration. Broad agreement exists to update archaic exclusion provisions, many of which are drawn in vague language. Dissatisfaction exists with the failure of the commission to act on this item despite detailed recommendations emanating from individual commissioners and legal staff. Finally, domestic group relations impacts seem to underlie the support for retention of country ceilings in some form to avoid concentration of immigrants in a few ethnic groups. Whether country ceilings can accomplish this—they have not since 1965—has yet to be frontally addressed.

REFUGEES

The major issues surrounding refugees are numbers, definition, first asylum, and resettlement. Another way to summarize the refugee issues is to say that the Cuban boatlift of 1980 raised questions about the adequacy of the 1980 refugee act.

Numbers—The numbers issue has been discussed previously. The concern is whether too many refugees have been admitted under the procedures of the 1980 refugee act, especially since there is no overall ceiling on total legal immigration.

Definition—The numbers concern spills over into the definitional issue. The 1980 refugee act expanded the U.S. definition beyond the criterion that one be from a Communist-dominated country or from the Middle East to the United Nations definition of persons persecuted or with a well-founded fear of persecution on the basis of race, religion, nationality, political opinion, or membership in a social group. The problem is one of interpretation. The bulk of the refugee admissions announced for the first two years under the 1980 refugee act are from Communist-dominated countries. Many wonder why Haitians have such a hard time gaining refugee status compared to Cubans, East Europeans, or people from the Soviet Union. It is not altogether clear that family reunion or economic motives are less important in movements from Communist countries. What persecution justifies the Reagan administration's seeking more refugee visas for Poles, for example, while Haitians are labeled as economic refugees?

The definitional problem was highlighted by the decision of President Carter in 1980 at the time of the "Mariel Boatlift" to declare that Haitian and Cuban boatpeople were not refugees, were not covered by the provisions of the 1980 refugee act, and therefore were allowed to be paroled into the United States despite the 1980 refugee act's specific prohibition of use of parole for refugee admissions. By definitional fiat, the Carter administration walked right around the 1980 refugee act. Perhaps it is time to recognize that the degree of government involvement in economies makes the political versus economic refugee distinction less and less workable. Another way of putting the same idea is to say that the interpretation of the "well-founded fear of persecution" is to a large extent a political decision (and has been in the past). Such an admission seems to violate genuine humanitarian values and calls for sensitivity and statesmanlike conduct that is not an everyday occurrence among politicians. Nevertheless, it may advance us beyond the sterility of definitional exercises.

The United States as a Country of First Asylum—The definitional problem exemplified by the unresolved Cuban/Haitian episode draws attention to an underlying flaw in U.S. refugee policy, namely the assumption that the United States would not be a country of first asylum. United States refugee policy has always been predicated on this country's being a country of resettlement and not a temporary haven for people who will be repatriated after stability returns. Nor, given the legislative enshrinement of the resettlement approach, has the United States seriously considered that we could best serve the cause of refugees —and even the U.S. national interest—by devoting more resources to care of refugees elsewhere in asylum countries and, therefore, reduce the number of refugees resettled in the United States and the resources expended on them. The current Southeast Asian situation would realistically mean that such a policy is for the medium or long term. Ideologically, it would require less emphasis on permanent settlement. Some would probably have a reaction similar to the widespread judgment of Japanese behavior vis-à-vis the Indo-Chinese, i.e., the attempt to fulfill obligations by a generous check with little or no acceptance of the people involved.

On the first-asylum issue, the commission went into great detail on program details to deal with mass movements of people seeking asylum but had nothing to say about policy on the issue. The assumption seemed to be that such movements would take place and reception centers and adjudication officers should be ready for activation. The involvement of state and local governments in resettlement planning was supported, and a policy of clustering was endorsed. Some specific policies on strict enforcement of eligibility for cash assistance and separation of medical from cash-assistance programs were also included in the recommendations. These program recommendations hardly added up to a policy statement of whether and under what conditions the United States should be a first asylum country.

Domestic Refugee Resettlement—The issue of resettlement strategies and obligations has become a bubbling cauldron of competing interests. The Indo-Chinese refugee resettlement, whose effects are still felt and unresolved, was a turning point in U.S. strategy.

Traditionally, voluntary agencies have resettled refugees in the United States. They acted for the United States in overseas processing and in domestic resettlement on a per capita fee basis through agreements with the U.S. Department of State. The agencies had great latitude in coordinating these activities among themselves. They also played a lobbying role in the development of legislative and administrative policy. The voluntary nature and humanitarian motivation, the need for private funds to supplement the government fees, the networks for sponsorship and resettlement, the presentation of citizens' views on who needed resettlement, the long experience of the major resettlement agencies dating back to the 1940s (and previously in some cases), and lack of any alternative (they were the "only game in town" for effective resettlement) all led to their unique role in U.S. policy and programs.

The decision to resettle tens, and eventually hundreds, of thousands of Indo-Chinese was not made as a result of ethnic lobbying through or coordinated by the voluntary agencies. The size of the resettlement led to an activist interagency task force to coordinate resettlement. State and local governments took active roles in sponsoring Indo-Chinese refugees and, therefore, got involved in resettlement to a degree that did not exist in prior movements. The problems of resettlement, especially the lack of regular and dependable funding; the problems of housing; the secondary migration within the United States to counter a policy of dispersion; the relative lack of ethnic Indo-Chinese infrastructure to cushion the impact (in contrast, for example, to Soviet Jews or Eastern Europeans after World War II); and the sheer numbers and problems of language training and job placement all led to pressures on Congress to restructure resettlement.

The 1980 refugee act provided for regular funding and called for federal responsibility for domestic resettlement to be located in the Department of Health and Human Services rather than in the Department of State. These moves led to requirements of state plans for resettlement and designation of state coordinators. State and local governments became more involved as entitlements to certain health and welfare benefits became more specific and generous but not fully funded by the federal government. (Some would say that increasing dependence on government grants rather than voluntary agency aid in resettlement has led to voluntary agencies' being referral services for refugee welfare and to a decline in refugee self-reliance, resulting in high levels of welfare dependency of Indo-Chinese refugees compared with previous groups.) The numbers, the concentration of refugees, and their presence in some states not used to large immigrant settlements reinforced state and local concern and involvement in refugee policy and practice. No longer could refugee policy and resettlement programs be left to the Department of State and voluntary agencies. In fact, the previous arrangements came to be seen as too cozy and lacking in accountability.

The degree and financing of special services to refugees (especially in light of local tax revolts and federal cutbacks) and the responsibility and influence in setting refugee policy and in program execution are all up in the air. The commission did not recommend an overall plan to resolve the dislocation in resettlement strategy precipitated by the Indo-Chinese experience and reinforced by the 1980 refugee act. Nor could it reasonably be expected to be otherwise. The resolution of refugee resettlement into a new institutionalized form to replace the prior Department of State voluntary organization axis will not result from recommendations by commissions. It is an ongoing political process that will involve many tests of strength from competing interests. Perhaps recognition of this fact will promote more realistic assessment of what is taking place and more enlightened options than efforts, like those of Peter the Great, to try to sort it all out and decree the shape of a bureaucratic resolution from the top.

In sum, the 1980 refugee act reinforced a set of social changes in refugee resettlement inaugurated by the Indo-Chinese experience. The 1980 act included a sunset provision requiring a review in three years of the executive-legislative consultative mechanism for development of refugee targets for each year. There seems to be no major opposition to the mechanism; the commission endorsed it. The major issues are whether refugees will be included in an overall cap on immigration, how to decide who is a refugee, and the ultimate resolution of fiscal and program responsibility for domestic resettlement.

WORKER MIGRATION

The issue of worker migration has already been considered previously. The relative weight to be accorded family and labor force needs is a basic tension in the area of selection criteria. Further, the need for a temporary labor program is debated. The debate includes not only the "need" for temporary workers (as opposed to the desire for them as a way to avoid structural adjustments or to forego profits) but also the part a temporary worker program can play in alleviating illegal migration pressures. Finally, the worker migration issue includes the debate over a policy of sanctioning employers and also questions about identification mechanisms so that employers can determine the work eligibility of job applicants.

Temporary Worker Programs—The first issue is whether temporary workers are needed. Those who respond negatively say that restructuring the economy and appropriate incentives will fill any so-called vacancies. They reject the notion that Americans will not take certain jobs. They will not take them if they are ill-paid, unsafe, and purposely kept insecure. The availability of temporary workers or illegal migrants only perpetuates the poor conditions, preventing structural adjustments. The United States does not have a labor shortage as Europe had after World War II or the Middle East oil exporters have now.

Supporters of a temporary worker program claim that labor autarchy implied by the previous arguments is a dream. The structural changes could not be accomplished overnight and could result in the loss of many jobs to foreign suppliers; they give no guarantee that certain jobs will still not be shunned (employers, after all, do not dictate social desirability), and they do not address regional availability of labor in a vast continental economy.

The commission recommended against a large temporary labor program but recommended continuation of the small-scale temporary worker program currently concentrated in eastern seaboard states (H-2 program). The Reagan Task Force, on the contrary, suggested a two-year trial program with a maximum of 50,000 visas a year.

Employer Sanctions—Some of the most vocal critics of a temporary worker program also oppose a sanctions program. Without sanctions, there will not be an effective bar to illegal migration, say sanctions supporters. Thus, they argue, opponents of temporary worker programs and sanctions cannot have it both ways unless they want to support illegal migration.

The sanctions issue ultimately revolves around a means for employers to determine work eligibility in a nondiscriminatory way. Employers can hardly be expected to make a complex, legal decision on who is and who is not an illegal alien. Without a universal identity system such checks are apt to be erroneous and discriminatorily made against persons with an accent or who "look foreign" to the employer. Hence some sort of identification seems necessary, whether an "upgraded" (hard to forge) social security card or a new work authorization card. Further, such a card must be shown by all job applicants—native or foreign born, citizen or alien—to avoid discrimination in job hiring, and records must be kept of the inspection of the document. The government cost to initiate and maintain a system, employer costs to inspect and record inspections of the document, and potential civil liberties problems of a universal identifier are all offered in opposition.

The Select Commission on Immigration and Refugee Policy sidestepped the issue by recommending sanctions and a secure means to enforce them but could not agree to support a specific means. The Reagan Task Force was equally vague. Referring to a defense for employers in sanction proceedings, the memorandum to the President of June 26, 1981, said: "Good faith reliance on existing documentation (including a more secure social security card) is a defense." President Reagan's immigration proposals supported employer sanctions with civil penalties (fines) and identification based on employer inspection of two means of identification chosen from birth certificate, driver's license, social security card, and draft registration.

Underlying the temporary worker and employer sanctions impasse is the disagreement over whether the United States needs workers and whether and to what extent such workers should be admitted as permanent residents or as temporary workers expected to leave after seasonal employment or after a specified period at work in a job of a permanent nature (but which can be filled by revolving personnel).

It should also be noted in this context that structural changes in the economy cannot be mandated from on high, certainly not in an economy like that of the United States. The demand for labor of certain sorts can be influenced by government policy but not dictated. Of course, all anyone really expects is a policy that can reduce illegal migration to manageable levels.

Finally, it can be briefly noted that there is broad agreement on many other policy thrusts to reduce the use of illegal migration as a means of meeting de facto labor demand. These include better management of the immigration service, more resources for border enforcement, more resources for labor law enforcement, foreign policy efforts to gain cooperation in control of illegal movement, and so on. However, specifics of such things as levels of funding and modes of cooperation are far from universally supported. The division over the need for workers is so wide that suggestions on these other topics are greeted warily as attempts to divert attention from the main issue—does the United States need workers and, if so, how should they be obtained.

DISTRIBUTIONAL EFFECTS OF IMMIGRATION

Immigration has distributional impacts. Regional population distribution is affected by migrant settlement patterns. Migrants do not disperse throughout the country in proportions equivalent to state populations. They are concentrated in Florida, the South-

west, and some of the traditional immigrant receiving areas of the
Northeast and North Central states. But all states have felt the
effects of immigration, if only due to the nation-wide Indo-Chinese
resettlement programs.

The regional distribution bears upon the issue of state and
local financing of services and the levels of federal reimburse-
ment. It should not be forgotten, however, that the presence of
immigrants of whatever sort may also be beneficial for local
economies due to consumption as well as a source of workers for
development where it is taking place (in Sunbelt areas, for example).

Finally, immigrant visas and refugee admissions are themselves a public good that is distributed. Who gets admitted or
rejected is a benefit or loss to relatives, employers, ethnic coalitions, or other interested parties. Decisions on the preference for
brothers and sisters of U.S. citizens has symbolic value as an
affirmation about whether ethnic cultures which honor extended
family ties are "American" enough to be recognized in law and to
receive a benefit. In the context of group relations, such symbolic
decisions are important.

Economic Forces Underlying International Migration

It is tempting to seek closure on such a complex issue as
immigration policy by limiting one's view to domestic political
differences. But the size and composition of migrant flows are
not only the result of unilateral national decisions on who may
enter a country. This issue has been examined by Alejandro
Portes of Johns Hopkins University, and my discussion is a summary of his analysis.

Today, flows of worker migration (and here I leave aside
refugee flows) are seen as the movement of a virtually inexhaustible supply of labor from developing to developed (or capital rich)
countries. It is part of exchanges among capitalist countries at
various levels of development. (Flows of manpower from or to
Communist countries are much smaller, and the dynamics are
different. They too are omitted here. The bulk of labor migrations are, nevertheless, included in this analysis.)

Inexhaustible supplies of labor are a relatively recent phenomenon. Labor shortages were endemic in the early modern

history of Europe and in colonization efforts. No exit policies were a regular feature of the early nation-states of Europe—although a contradiction, and often an expensive one for expelling nations, existed with expulsion of religious or other minorities. American colonization by Europeans was primarily a means of exploiting resources, especially land. Labor was in short supply. Coerced labor of native Indians failed. Indentured servitude of Europeans produced insufficient numbers. Slavery was used to develop cash crop agriculture.

Industrialization in the nineteenth century required additional labor, and changed ideology about slavery required new sources. European agriculturalists displaced by technological change were involved enough in a money economy to respond to wages, but the cost of movement and the risk created a need for active recruitment to mobilize and transfer labor. Indentured servitude was still used, especially by England, which brought Indian workers from Asia to Africa and the Caribbean.

The current situation is the result of historically specific circumstances. The question is why certain flows take place, why certain areas are among the senders or receivers, while others which seem similar in major ways are not.

Both orthodox modernization theories and dependency theories converge on a push-pull explanation. Backwardness and poverty of sending areas and the gap between them and receiving areas explain the movements. Lists of pushes and pulls, emphasizing one or the other, depending on perspective, are all *post factum* explanations. Nor do they answer the question of why certain areas and not others send or receive migrants.

Attempts to explain specific flows in terms of recruitment are not germaine to many contemporary movements. Recent Dominican movement to New York City or Bolivian and Paraguayan movement to Buenos Aires seem to have had no recruitment component. The nineteenth century recruitment that brought workers to America was a historically conditioned mechanism. Theories of social networks explain the continuation and expansion of flows but not their genesis.

Contrary to the conclusions of orthodox modernization and dependency theories from economics, current migrations include not just rural migrants and agricultural workers or even the poorest, the unemployed, and the marginalized of the developing societies. Profiles of international migrants from many sources reaffirm the mix of urban and rural backgrounds, the fact that the spectrum of occupations is covered, that it is not those on the margins but those with jobs, experience, and some resources who dominate the international labor flows.

What underlies these patterns is the incorporation of developing economies into the international system, the development of aspirations and tastes which cannot be met at home, and the capacity to produce more workers with the training and experience appropriate for modern sector employment than can be absorbed, whether it be physicians, skilled, or semiskilled workers. These factors mobilize workers for migration to industrialized economies. This process explains internal movement to investment centers and growth areas as well as international migration.

How mobilized a work force is for international migration seems dependent on strategies for development. Export-led development, being most integrated with the world system (aspirations and tastes high), and relying on high technology and/or low wages (and, therefore, lack of jobs and/or low wages to meet those aspirations and tastes), is most conducive to migration. Import substitution to develop and widen internal markets is less prone to labor export. An import substitution strategy that is based not on quantitative expansion of the internal market but qualitative substitution of foreign technology to produce domestically the same durable and nondurable goods leads to the same result as export-led growth strategies.

In short, a development strategy that spreads access to goods, with a lower import content in manufacture, higher value added per unit of wage, greater dispersion of wealth, and less exposure to consumer tastes of industrialized countries, will reduce the migration potential. Outward looking economies based on export-led growth least meet these requirements.

For receiving countries, absolute labor shortages, the competitive sectors of the economy (small manufacturing, for example) sometimes kept alive by tariff and nontariff barriers to trade, especially from developing countries, and the existence of many socially undesirable jobs even in an advanced economy explain the attraction. Large-scale expansions as in postwar Europe or the Middle East after 1973 are examples of labor shortage. The latter two reasons (competitive sector need for low wages and socially undersirable jobs) explain the existence of temporary labor programs and illegal migration in many developed countries. The continued movement is also due in some part to social and kin networks reuniting families of former migrants.

International worker migration is set in motion and sustained, therefore, by forces usually outside the domain of immigration policy per se. In analyses of immigration policy options and their domestic impact (on group relations, for example), it is well to bear in mind that domestic political decisions about immigration do not operate in a vacuum. Immigration issues are part and parcel of the international economic system of transfers of capital and goods and are affected by the development strategies adopted by or forced upon developing countries.

Robert C. Weaver

3

The Impact of Ethnicity
upon Urban America

Introduction

The economic, racial, and residential patterns of urban areas have changed drastically since World War II. With these changes the problems of cities—revenue, delivery of services, safety, transportation, and intergroup relations—have become more difficult and complex. In all of this there is a constant interface of people and structure, providing an analogy with the controversy over assimilation versus ethnicity, where the interface is often between structure and culture.

The Urban Condition

By the 1970s it was clear that urban America was troubled. Many, but not all, central cities faced real financial difficulties dramatized by the well-publicized threat of bankruptcy to New

ROBERT C. WEAVER *is a distinguished professor emeritus of Urban Affairs at Hunter College, The City University of New York. He has been in public service for forty-eight years, including administrator of the Housing and Home Finance Agency under President John F. Kennedy and secretary of the Department of Housing and Urban Development under President Lyndon B. Johnson. Dr. Weaver has written four books and over 175 articles. He holds thirty honorary degrees.*

York. There was no universal urban crisis, but there were crises and threats of crises in many older cities, primarily in the Northeast and Midwest while many cities in the Sunbelt were prospering. The pattern was not entirely regional but was structural as well. This was reflected in the fact that some of the older southern cities had problems, too. What seemed to be universal were the adverse effects of isolation of core cities as they became a relatively small segment of their total metropolitan area.

EVOLUTION OF THE PROBLEM CITY

The basic source of the cities' most pressing difficulties had been long in the making. It involved population movement which initially occurred primarily within the city borders and had no noticeable adverse impact upon the revenue or the economic health of the city. More recently, urban population movement brought about a new economic role for cities. In the past, large cities had had an advantaged position. While facing increasing expenditure responsibilities, they also had the greatest concentration of fiscal resources which provided an impressive tax base. Included were significant concentrations of retail and other economic activities of prosperous and growing central business districts, expansion of manufacturing, and constant growth of commercial and residential construction. A broad spectrum of the population, including the more affluent, resided within the city's borders, albeit usually in separate areas. By the post–World War II period, when there was a rash of new family formation and an unprecedented volume of suburban residential construction, this had clearly changed.

The central cities attempted to continue their basic functions. But many of the suburban settlements which expanded especially after World War II had little in common with the suburb as it had been. They differed both in function and form and, most importantly, in their vast scale. A new type of human settlement evolved. It was, in effect, an outer city wrapped around the old city, living in uneasy proximity to the latter, linked by surviving governmental, utility, communication, and banking networks, but relatively independent socially, culturally, and economically.

Economic and Structural Woes—Cities' expenditure responsibilities dramatically increased in recent years as they received and retained a disproportionate share of unskilled labor for which there was decreasing demand and to whom society became committed to provide public assistance. Concurrently, the cities have suffered a drastic decline in their relative resources, as they experienced the outward movement of the more affluent and a large sector of the middle class, as well as of retail trade, industry, and, ultimately, commercial activities. The older high tax-producing central business districts increasingly accommodated new functions, such as government and other tax exempt activities, at the same time that most older cities could no longer annex adjacent metropolitan areas. The volume of employment declined, and the tax base of many cities eroded.

As crucial as these economic problems and their social counterparts proved to be, they were not the only major disabilities of core cities. In the suburb the operative words became proliferation, fragmentation, and scatteration. There was a proliferation of governments into tiny suburban enclaves and special districts which were incapable of dealing with metropolitan-wide problems. What resulted was a diffusion of small political entities, rivaled only by the frequent scatteration of land use patterns which, in turn, devoured desirable agricultural land, occasioned wasteful use of urban land, required unnecessarily costly infrastructure, and gave rise to duplicative administrative expenditures.

The Roles of Ethnic Groups in the Economy

Understanding recent developments concerning America's ethnic groups requires familiarity with their historical roles. Basic to this is the realization that until comparatively recently the indigenous population has been insufficient to meet the nation's labor requirements. In colonial America the primary need was for agricultural workers. In the South the source was black slaves; elsewhere it was predominantly European immigrants; in the Southwest increasing dependence was subsequently placed upon Mexican-Americans. By the nineteenth century there was a severe shortage of industrial workers, and the volume of European immigration soared, even as virgin land continued to be brought into cultivation by small-scale farmers, including many immigrants. Allocation of one billion acres of public land greatly accelerated the process.

EUROPEAN IMMIGRANTS

The saga of European immigration is part of American folk-lore. It is so deeply ingrained in our tradition that many, including the descendants of immigrants, assume it is the classic and universal experience of those who migrated to American cities. But this has not been the case. Thus it is important to delineate the circumstances, in addition to the obvious one of absence of intense color prejudice, which was basic to the European immigrants' upward mobility in rural and urban areas. Three elements are important. The first is that most immigrants who entered agriculture did so either initially as independent farmers or with the expectation, frequently realized, of soon becoming so. The second is that in the earlier phases of American industrialization there was not only receptiveness to skilled and semi-skilled immigrants, but also great demand for unskilled labor, enabling those with rural backgrounds to join the armies engaged in mining, construction, and manufacturing. Finally, even those immigrants initially relegated to unskilled jobs were concentrated in the most dynamic centers of the economy. Temporally and physically these immigrant workers were positioned in line for early upgrading to semiskilled and skilled positions. As this occurred, the stereotypes associated with their dress, language, customs, and other habits waned.

BLACK AMERICANS

After an unsuccessful attempt to enslave the Indians and an abortive experience with indentured servants, the South turned to African slaves. Soon both regional and national vested interests in the peculiar institution developed as cotton became the economic base of the South and the American export staple. Not only did slavery deny blacks freedom, citizenship, equality before the law, mobility, and compensation for their labor, but it also produced a rationalization which characterized them as sub-human. Thus even free blacks were virtually slaves without masters. Blacks were said to occupy a lower plane in the evolutionary scale, to lapse into indolence as they reached adulthood, to be endowed with traits associated with beasts of burden, to be childlike and good natured but given to fits of passion and acts of singular atrocity. This summary, incidentally, is not based upon the extensive proslavery tracts published and widely disseminated in the eighteenth and nineteenth centuries. It is a characterization of "the Negro" which appeared in the 1911 *Encyclopedia Britannica,* half a century after emancipation.

Slaves were almost exclusively a rural people tied to plantations. They had practically no exposure to education and almost as little industrial experience, although they became the artisans of the self-contained plantation economy and of many southern cities. With emancipation they remained primarily tied to the land by labor contracts which, when combined with vagrancy laws, Black Codes, and the bias of southern courts, relegated most of them to peonage.

In the half century after the Civil War, when more than 24 million immigrants entered the United States, 90 percent of American blacks remained in the South. They were almost universally denied access to public land and were excluded from industry at the very time that it had an enormous capacity to absorb peasant labor. This was also a period when blacks were systematically relegated to second-class citizenship in all aspects of American life. Even in the North, there were significant differences in the occupational distribution between blacks and the new southern, central, and eastern European immigrants. Stanley Lieberson in *A Piece of the Pie: Blacks and White Immigrants Since 1880* presents detailed census data which demonstrate that at the turn of the twentieth century, in the lower occupational ranges where they competed, blacks were more concentrated in service jobs and the new Europeans in manufacturing jobs. "There is also strong evidence that the black pattern in the North resembled very much the pattern found in the urban South. . . ." In the late nineteenth and early twentieth centuries, blacks were caught in the cross fire between unions which excluded them because of color and periodic utilization as strikebreakers.

It was not until the cessation of European immigration at the outbreak of World War I that blacks significantly entered American industry. Like most peasant labor reserves, they were relegated primarily to unskilled work. Paradoxically, their advent accelerated the occupational upgrading of European immigrants already well underway. Blacks were soon adversely affected by two structural developments. The first was the Great Depression which occasioned disproportionately high rates of unemployment for them both because of color and because of their lack of seniority and their low occupational status. The second was the beginning of a decline in the economy's long-term need for unskilled labor. Thus many blacks became marginal workers and the group's upgrading was further delayed. Blacks did, however, retain a somewhat precarious foothold in the nation's industrial machine.

World War II provided a breakthrough in upward occupational mobility. By the end of hostilities, semiskilled, single-skilled, and a smaller number of skilled jobs were opened to blacks. The 1960s brought equal employment opportunity executive orders and legislation, culminating in affirmative action. In the wake of these developments, the earlier concentration of blacks in agricultural labor and domestic service was altered. Urbanization and industrial employment had increased the scope of occupations available to black men and women. There was a rise of a new middle class and significant expansion of white-collar jobs in the growing service industries and public agencies. For the first time the black middle class was no longer concentrated in the ghetto, moving toward the mainstream occupational structure, although often providing services primarily to other blacks.

But there remained a sizable black underclass, whose existence showed how far the group was behind the economic status of earlier entrants into the urban economy. Nor was there lack of job discrimination against well-trained minority people. Striking evidence of this has been set forth by Bernard E. Anderson and Phoebe H. Cottingham in the spring 1981 issue of *Daedalus*, devoted to *American Indians, Blacks, Chicanos, and Puerto Ricans*:

> Some recent studies of minorities in the lower market show that disparities in educational attainment between minorities and others are narrowing. Yet minority employment status and earnings appear to be converging with those of other U.S. workers at a slower pace than educational achievement.

So despite the fact that the civil rights movement of the 1950s and 1960s brought a dramatic reduction in the long reign of widespread terror in the South and bestowed full citizenship rights to blacks under the law, including voting rights, there was and remains unfinished business for democracy.

Roots of Ethnicity—Failure to gain equal access to the mainstream of the American economy created great disillusionment among many blacks, especially youth who had lived through the civil rights campaign. Some became extremely hostile. For them there was only one route—to look inward and develop group strength and institutions. Others, including many who had laid the groundwork for and participated in the civil rights campaign, did not embrace a racial ethnicity which glorified separatism, although most of them, too, found a new pride in greater recognition of African and black history. They considered separatism a withdrawal or retreat, a futile attempt to avoid the reality of life in America and a policy which offered little hope of providing a solid economic base for blacks.

Whatever ideological differences about separatism (or the lesser amount about affirmative action, most of which focuses on methods), there is near unanimity concerning the primacy of securing equal opportunity and concerning the responsibility of government to press for equality and justice.

NATIVE AMERICANS

Native Americans (Indians) and Mexican-Americans had extensive ancestral claims to the land and its resources. From the beginning of the colonization of America and increasingly as the West was settled, the thirst of whites for Indian and Mexican land increased. At the beginning, however, the relative strength of the Native Americans and the colonists' dependence upon them forced the whites to recognize Indians as independent powers and to negotiate land treaties with them. Initially there was some ambiguity about whites' reaction to Indians: they seemed to be somewhat glamorous; but as the appetite for their land increased and they resisted its expropriation, meeting force with force, the nation sought a justification for land grabbing. What resulted was the concept of the Indian as a savage who did not really use properly or productively the land to which he claimed title. His conquest became national policy, involving as well his uprooting and banishment to reservations. Simultaneously attempts were made to destroy his culture. Neither this effort nor the impact of conquest and environmental factors which at first threatened his decimation succeeded in eliminating the Indian. For a time, however, the decimation seemed about to occur. It is estimated, for example, that in 1491 some 12 to 15 million Indians were north of the Rio Grande; the census of 1910 reported only 210,000. In 1980, the figure was 1,362,000

The treaties between the United States and Indian nations certified that the latter had existed as self-governing entities prior to their contact with Europeans. These treaties had, and continue to have, great significance for the self-image and cultural traditions of Native Americans. But the treaties were soon violated. With little employment possibilities on the reservations, Indians have sought work elsewhere. Since World War II, an increasing number of youth have migrated to such metropolitan centers as Los Angeles, Minneapolis, the Bay Area, Seattle, Denver, New York, and Buffalo. Almost half of all Indians could be classified as urban by 1981.

Two recent events may improve the economic status of Native Americans. First, there has been an intensification of litigation to recover indemnity for, or title to, the lands they were guaranteed under earlier treaties, and there have been significant victories. Secondly, in this period of resource scarcity, the deposits of oil, gas, and minerals on what was thought to be land of little worth when it was designated as Indian reservations bid fair to have untold value. Certainly they should alleviate some of the poverty which has long haunted the Native American.

Neither Indian boarding schools removed from reservations nor adult residence in urban centers remote from reservations has succeeded in severing the strong ties Indians have to their cultural heritage. Theirs is not a monolithic culture expressed in a single language. Rather it is described as a culture of many tribes united by a single tradition—survival. The affluence which seems to be in the offing will mean that some Indians will become even more prone to make it alone. They are committed to self-determination on a tribal basis and to just compensation for land which was confiscated from them. According to Michael A. Dorris, writing in the cited issue of *Daedalus*, these are their aspirations rather than equal access to the mainstream of America.

MEXICAN-AMERICANS

Like Indians, Mexican-Americans were conquered. Again, land
was the issue. And their treatment was overshadowed by that of the
Indian in semantics as well as in deeds. For once the white man
lusted after their land, he began to designate them as aboriginal
Indians. Then he provoked a war with Mexico and forced that
nation to cede over half of its territory to the United States.
Nearly 80,000 Mexicans lived in the area involved, and most of
them elected to become citizens of this country under a treaty
which guaranteed their property rights. As with Indians, Mexicans were dispossessed of their land through chicanery and out-
right violence. Augmented by immigration, the Mexican-American
population increased, and soon it was the Southwest's labor
reserve.

By the turn of the twentieth century, Mexican-Americans, for
the most part, had become landless laborers, politically and
economically impotent, subject to violence, and in some places
relegated to segregated schools. At that time they began to enter
the lower ranges of industrial employment, enjoying very little
mobility out of unskilled and semiskilled occupations. In the
rural areas, a sizable ethnic wage differential continued to exist.
Everywhere their employment status was marginal; they were the
first fired when there was economic contraction and were utilized
as a sort of strike insurance. The small middle class was generally firmly rooted in a segregated economy and society. By
the early 1920s, Mexicans began to settle outside the Southwest.
As with blacks, they were recruited by heavy industries, such as
iron and steel, meat packing, and automobile assembly, largely
in the Midwest. About 15 percent had left the Southwest by
1930. A similarly more dispersed pattern developed for farm
labor. Part of these population movements were in response to
the labor shortage occasioned by World War I.

Although there are no exact figures on Mexican migration,
there is evidence that it was substantial. These circumstances
resulted from de facto and unrestricted movement across the
border between Mexico and the United States. It is estimated
that about a quarter of a million Mexicans arrived in this country
during the first three decades of the twentieth century. Included

were many of the professionals, entrepreneurs, landowners, and intellectuals who had been displaced by the Mexican Revolution of 1910. In 1924 there was an adverse reaction to European immigration. Even with the passage of the 1924 immigration act, the drive for racial purity which swept the country at the time, and the denigration of the racial mixture so prevalent in Latin America and in Indian nations such as Mexico, no effective action was taken to curb Mexican immigration. The reason seems to have been the Southwest's need for cheap labor and the generally subservient status of Mexicans.

Like other minorities, Mexican-Americans suffered from the depression with great intensity. Already marginal before its impact, they were particularly vulnerable. The most cruel aspect was the forced and indiscriminate repatriation inflicted upon them. It has been estimated, for example, that between 1929 and 1934 more than 400,000 Mexicans were required to leave the country under "voluntary repatriation." Indigence, not citizenship, was the criterion used in selection for repatriation.

World War II led to some significant changes. In 1942 there was a program based on the 1917–20 bilateral agreement between Mexico and this country designed to supply agricultural labor. Those involved stayed in this country for a limited time, usually the harvest season. The United States underwrote travel costs, insured a minimum wage, and guaranteed just and equitable treatment. The program was extended annually, and it was legally formalized in 1951. When it was terminated thirteen years later, annual immigration quotas of 120,000 were established for all the nations of the Western Hemisphere. Between 4 and 5 million Mexicans entered the United States under the program, and of course there were abuses. Also a steady flow of undocumented workers paralleled those who entered via the bilateral agreement. The former, not restricted to agricultural labor, increasingly sought employment in the cities. These abuses and collateral developments merit analysis as we contemplate an immigration program for "guest workers."

Two circumstances shaped urban residential patterns for Mexican-Americans in a mold somewhat different from that of blacks or Puerto Ricans. In many cities of the Southwest, Mexicans were among the original founders and thus had access to desirable areas. Also, in recent years cities in the Sunbelt often grew by annexation, and the areas annexed frequently included traditionally Mexican settlements. In short, residential segregation of Mexican-Americans, while often the pattern, has never been as prevalent or rigid as that of blacks and Puerto Ricans.

The volume of Mexican-American employment—especially at lower classifications—grew appreciably during the post–World War II era. The group's urban population was and remains dominated by younger people, and it has achieved national recognition because of high fertility rates and continuing dispersion. By the outset of the 1980s, Mexican-Americans (or Chicanos, as they increasingly are called) were 60 percent of the nation's Hispanic population.

In 1981, Leobardo F. Estrada, F. Chris Garcia, Reynaldo Flores Macias, and Lionel Maldonado wrote in the spring issue of *Daedalus:*

> Jobs are available to Mexican migrants, largely in the secondary labor market, where the lack of fringe benefits makes these low-paying, seasonal jobs unattractive to domestic workers.

> Mexicans—particularly without legal rights and privileges—are especially desirable for agribusiness, marginal industries, seasonal work or in business quickly affected by economic downturns.

Roots of Ethnicity—In the wake of the civil rights movement of the 1960s, a rash of Chicano activist organizations appeared. Many were critical of American society: some advocated socialism; others strove to set up various types of alternative or separatist institutions. The paper drawn upon above stated:

> They were looking, in short, for a radical and equitable transformation of a racist society. Almost all such groups emphasized the distinctiveness of Mexican culture. They actively promoted Chicano cultural norms and values. Chicano culture represented the common ground that bound together all the members of the group.

Charismatic leaders emerged and gave direction and zest to economic, political, and educational programs. At first there was confrontation, but it was generally short-lived, leaving, however, a heritage of more political activity. The greatest and perhaps the most permanent impact has been in education. There was much ideological diversity among the student groups; some stressed apprenticeship training in community-based and campus-based politics. Some turned to union organization off campus, but most joined in pressing for increased recruitment of Chicano students and faculty, as well as for curricula more relevant to Chicano concerns. One of the consequences was a significant increase in the number of Mexican-American lawyers, physicians, teachers, and business managers. Another was the rise of an emphasis upon group consciousness. And the constant influx of illegal aliens across the U.S.-Mexican border enables Mexican-Americans to replenish their cultural strength if they desire to do so. This movement from Mexico also keeps alive resentment of *gringo* imperialism which has long been delineated and resented in the homeland.

PUERTO RICANS

Because of the free access to the United States labor market extended to Puerto Ricans when in World War I they were granted citizenship, it is difficult to arrive at firm figures on their migration to the mainland. Yet it seems clear that before 1920 only a miniscule number of persons born on the island had migrated to the mainland. Between 1920 and 1978, some 934,000 born in Puerto Rico entered the United States.

This migration has been characterized by the following features:

1. a recent growth in returning to Puerto Rico;
2. some dispersal of Puerto Rican concentration but continuing clustering in New York City and the Northeast;
3. after 1974 a sharp drop in the number of farm workers coming to the mainland for seasonal work under contracts between the Commonwealth government and the East Coast Growers Association but continuing traffic to noncontract growers; and
4. growth of Puerto Rican population on the mainland through natural reproduction in excess of the growth attributed to migration. (Since 1950 the population of Puerto Ricans in the mainland has nearly doubled each decade; in 1980, there were some 1.8 million Puerto Ricans in the United States.)

In addition to the handicaps of language and (for many) of color, Puerto Ricans, as blacks to a slightly lesser degree, have been adversely affected by the economic decline and the financial woes of the urban areas where they are concentrated. They first entered industrial employment in significant numbers on the mainland a generation after blacks and Chicanos had done so. When they did, American industries' need for, and capacity to absorb, unskilled labor had reached a new low. Some of the consequences of this and of discrimination, especially for the darker component, were high rates of unemployment, casual employment, slow rates of occupational upgrading, and educational problems for youth. By 1980, unemployment among teenagers was disastrously high, and one-fourth of Puerto Ricans left school by the time they were sixteen; over 70 percent were no longer enrolled by age nineteen. Many mainland Puerto Rican teenagers were not enrolled in school; they were working or more probably looking for work.

During the mid-1970 recession, the proportion of older mainland Puerto Ricans looking for work was 1.5 times that for the total U.S. population. Similar disparities existed for teenagers, women, and men beginning work careers. The jobs most Puerto Ricans have are in slow-growth industries, entail periodic layoffs, and are greatly diminishing in the cities where Puerto Ricans continue to live. While young Puerto Ricans are shifting from factory to service occupations, the latter jobs are often casual, mostly devoid of potential for upgrading, and low paying. Older Puerto Ricans similarly displaced often turn to manual labor, which provides less security and lower wages.

In 1981, the median income for white families was $21,900; for Hispanics, $14,720; and for blacks, $12,690. An earlier census report based upon a sample taken in March 1980 estimated that Cubans had the highest incomes among Hispanics; Mexican-Americans earned 87 percent as much, and Puerto Ricans, 70 percent. Almost 40 percent of Puerto Rican families were estimated by the Census Bureau as living below the poverty line in 1976–77. This contrasts with 23.1 percent for all families of Spanish descent (Hispanics) and 8.7 percent for those of non-Spanish origin. Despite the failure of most median family income figures to take into account age, size, education, skill, region, and volume of employment, they do yield a rough measure of relative standard of living among the ethnic groups involved. Employment data, especially those for similar age and sex categories as in the instance of teenagers' unemployment cited subsequently, are a more reliable index of groups' economic status.

Roots of Ethnicity—There are many explanations and manifestations of ethnicity among Puerto Ricans. A basic element is the relationship between the island and the mainland. This occasions criticism of the economic and political status of Puerto Rico and finds expression in the continuing controversy over statehood. This last issue has expression in a class-oriented approach to the economic and, to a degree, the political future of the island.

Frank Bonilla and Ricardo Campos, writing in *Daedalus* in 1981, spoke of "the Puerto Rican Tradition: the awareness of being a people set apart and denied, a people whose unfilled economic and political aspirations are in the main simply excluded from consideration within present social arrangements." And they added, "More than ever, those who would lead minority peoples need to see clearly the connections between internal events and the long history of colonialism and present patterns of economic and political domination on a world scale."

The constant movement of Puerto Ricans from the island to the mainland and vice versa via a plane trip of a few hours occasions unique consequences. It provides Puerto Ricans on the mainland ready access to a homeland. The conditions at each destination are known at the other; this serves to maintain further the migrants' ties with the island. It replenishes the presence and influence of Spanish in all aspects of social life. For some intellectuals it is the basis of identifying the culture of poverty with both locales and with a dominant economic system which affects each. Even as Puerto Ricans increase their command of English they do not abandon their native Spanish. Juan Flores, John Attinasi, and Pedro Pedraza, Jr., made this observation in *Daedalus:*

> In contrast to the traditional pattern of transition from the foreign language to English over three generations, with grandparents and grandchildren being virtually monolingual in one or the other language, nearly all Puerto Ricans are bilingual to some degree, with second language skills acquired, for the most part, outside any formal language instruction. . . .
>
> Effective ghettoization, the sinister real-life reflex of ethnic pluralisms, is a major objective factor in the seemingly enigmatic maintenance of

Spanish even among third-generation and fourth-generation Puerto Ricans in the United States.

Ethnicity among European Ethnics and Minorities

Deemphasis of the concept of the melting pot has distinctly different implications for those groups which have "made it" in the United States and those which have tried unsuccessfully to do so. For the successful it implies, among other things, that their upward mobility has been due basically to innate ability and/or traditions and culture. A corollary is that groups still generally outside the mainstream are so situated because of the absence of the attributes which account primarily for the first group's much more favorable status. Repudiation of the melting pot theory on the part of those who find it inapplicable to their experience says, in effect, that acceptance into the system was and is not such a big deal after all, since the system is not that good.

In both instances there is intellectual emphasis upon ethnic consciousness and its vigorous advocacy. But as Stephen Steinberg observed in his book, *The Ethnic Myth: Race, Ethnicity, and Class in America:*

> Although both groups expressed a common impulse to raise ethnic consciousness and strengthen group bonds, there was a fundamental difference between them, rooted in the fact that racial minorities are generally poorer and must cope with a more intense and pervasive bigotry based on indelible marks of race. That the ethnic resurgence involved more than nostalgia became clear as racial minorities and white ethnics became polarized on a series of issues relating to schools, housing, local government, and control over federal programs. Given the different economic and political dimensions of ethnicity in the two instances, it would not be correct to treat the ethnicity of racial minorities and immigrant white minorities as variations of the same phenomenon.

For descendants of European immigrants, ethnicity is often, in part, a self-flattering explanation of their economic, political, and social advancement in the New World. It is, however, not a complete fabrication, since ethnic groups do have unique and significant characteristics; but it is something of a distortion because it greatly underestimates economic and social structural explanations. For major racial minorities, ethnicity is, in part, an expression of frustration and hostility.

With the exception of Indians, a major concern of these groups has been for equal rights and greater access to economic opportunity. Some Chicanos seem to believe that one day Mexico may influence meaningfully their destiny in the United States; some Puerto Ricans seem to believe that Latin America will do so for them both on the mainland and the island. Here there appears to be a parallel with romantic strains in the ethnicity among descendants of European immigrants.

Ethnicity has more realistic goals when it is targeted to foster group consciousness and self-help while instilling a new kind of collective group understanding and pride. Its negative aspects are chauvinism, which by implication downgrades other groups, or escapism, which discourages realistic self-analysis. The desirable stance is a balance between structure and culture in analyzing a group's success or failure. As Orlando Patterson has suggested, "Structural and cultural explanations are not mutually exclusive." Nor is it necessary "that culture always be viewed as casually secondary—not only that it is ultimately so."

Recent Changes in Urban Residential Ethnic Patterns

The 1980 census population figures had been awaited expectantly by students of ethnic population movements. While they do reflect significant trends, they are flawed in several respects. First, it has long been recognized that the census materially underenumerates urban blacks. Also the census category "Hispanics" is somewhat misleading. It actually encompasses primarily Mexican-Americans, Puerto Ricans, and Cubans—groups, among other smaller components, which have a common original language but also significant economic and social differences. Earlier discussions of family income and ethnicity among the major component groups reflected wide variations at the same time that the peculiar urban residential patterns of Mexican-Americans were delineated. Subsequent passages will call attention to striking variations in the rates of suburbanization and lesser ones in unemployment among the major subgroups. Clearly, therefore, economic and social data for Hispanics do not imply the same degree of solidarity reflecting status or attitudes as comparable data for blacks. Census data for Hispanics are especially unreliable and inconsistent over time as indicators of the racial composition of the group identified as Hispanics. For example, in

1980, 55 percent of those so classified identified themselves as white and 40 percent as "other" on the race question. In 1970, some 90 percent of those of Mexican-American, Cuban, and other Spanish-speaking descent were counted as white. Finally, the 1980 census greatly undercounted the large number of illegal aliens, especially from Mexico.

THE LOSS OF WHITES IN CITIES

The 1980 census figures showed an enormous migration of whites from the nation's largest cities and a majority or substantial minority of blacks or blacks and Hispanics combined in eight of the twenty-six largest cities. The number of blacks increased between 1970 and 1980 only moderately in most of the big cities and declined in some. Because of a larger decrease in white population, however, blacks were a majority in Baltimore, New Orleans, and Detroit, as well as in Atlanta and Washington where they had held that status in 1970. Black majorities also existed in some smaller cities, such as Newark, Gary, Birmingham, Wilmington, and Richmond; they were almost a majority in St. Louis and Memphis. Blacks and Hispanics combined exceeded the number of whites in Chicago, while in Los Angeles and Houston, blacks, Hispanics, and "others" exceeded the white population.

The 1980 census documented the belief that Hispanics are the nation's fastest-growing minority group. They are now a majority of the population in San Antonio, and it is likely that they either do or soon will outnumber blacks in New York, Los Angeles, San Diego, Phoenix, San Francisco, and Denver. Hispanics are increasingly dispersed, although with the exception of New York, where Puerto Ricans are the core element, and Miami, where Cubans dominate, the numbers involved outside the Southwest are small as compared to that of blacks in the metropolitan areas. The increase in "other" census racial minorities, primarily American Indians and Asians, varied widely between regions and cities. It was substantial in California and the Southwest. The largest urban concentration of "other" racial groups was in New York City; Los Angeles and Chicago, too, had a substantial number.

These ethnic changes in the urban population occurred in a

setting in which the number and ratio of racial minorities in the national population increased significantly. Blacks, Hispanics, Asians, Pacific Islanders, American Indians, and a small number of others grew from 12.5 percent in 1970 to 16.8 percent in 1980. Some Sunbelt cities, such as San Diego, San Jose, San Antonio, and Phoenix, departed from the national trend and registered an increase in white population. This was due, in large part, to their ability to annex suburban territory.

SUBURBANIZATION OF BLACKS

As is generally recognized, suburbanization of blacks in the last decade involved primarily the middle class. In some metropolitan areas, largely where there was a somewhat limited black population, some more affluent blacks lived in relatively integrated communities around the suburban perimeters. Where there were large concentrations of blacks, the tendency was for substantial middle-class black subdivisions to appear in one or more corridors beyond the core areas, representing replication of classic patterns of racial succession in neighborhoods. Regardless of spatial distribution, the outward movement of primarily higher-income blacks accentuated the concentration of the poor in the inner city.

In short, blacks have increased in numbers and as a percentage of the total population in the suburbs of most large cities over the last decade at the same time that whites were moving into virtually all-white areas of new growth and prosperity either in the suburban rings or, more frequently, beyond metropolitan areas. This paralleled the entrance of blacks into suburbs, many of which were declining economically and in population growth. But, as in the case of earlier racial changes in neighborhoods within the central cities, the move usually occasioned upgrading the quality of shelter.

In some cities, such as Cleveland, St. Louis, Philadelphia, Newark, Washington, and San Francisco, where the number of blacks declined over the decade, black movement to the suburbs seemed almost as intense as that of whites in previous decades. In thirty-eight metropolitan areas with populations of a million or more, the percentages of blacks in the suburbs increased from 4.7 to 6.5 between 1970 and 1980. For the forty-one metropolitan areas of 500,000 to one million population, the number of blacks in the suburbs increased by 25 percent, while their proportion of the total suburban population declined somewhat. This was especially true in the South, representing primarily the replacement or outnumbering of blacks who lived in former rural areas that were becoming suburban.

The 1980 figures indicated that more than half, or 14.7 million, of the nation's blacks lived in the central cities of metropolitan areas, while 6 million additional blacks resided in the suburbs and rural fringes of those areas. Some 20 percent of blacks lived in suburbs, constituting 6 percent of the population, where they were increasing faster than in the cities. The number of blacks in the South increased substantially with the great decline in black migration out of the region and a small influx from the North. Their proportion of the total population of the South declined, however, as there was a surge of whites moving into that now generally prospering region. Blacks, however, were not moving to the West where new jobs in mining, recreation, and energy were providing a bonanza of growth and prosperity.

At the same time, despite the reverse movement of blacks back to the South, they remained a large numerical and proportionate sector of the urban population in the Northeast and Midwest where there was marked decline in economic activity, especially in industries and occupations in which blacks had been heavily concentrated. As noted above, Puerto Ricans, who remained highly concentrated in the Northeast, suffered from the same structural situation.

SUBURBANIZATION OF HISPANICS

The rate of suburbanization of Hispanics was much greater than that of blacks. And a much larger proportion of lower-income households was involved. About half of the 14.8 million Hispanics counted by the 1980 census lived in central cities, and more than 5 million, or 37 percent, lived in suburbs and rural fringes of cities. The rest were in rural counties, mostly in the Southwest. Among those who lived in the suburbs, as would be expected from their numerical preponderance, the vast majority were Mexican-Americans primarily in the Southwest and West. But more was involved since the proportions of the major subgroups among Hispanics in the suburbs varied widely. The more affluent Cubans evidenced the greatest predilection for suburban living, the Mexican-Americans significantly less, and the Puerto Ricans only half as much as the Mexican-Americans. In 1978 the proportions living in the suburbs and rural fringes were 60.2 percent, 34.3 percent, and 16.2 percent respectively.

It is doubtful that the census figure of 37 percent for Hispanics in the suburbs represents a significant decline in their absolute number in the cities. This could be true because of the extremely high natural increase rate in the population of Spanish-speaking people in the nation and the failure of the census to enumerate the large number of illegal aliens, who increasingly were gravitating to the cities.

Recent movement of low-income Hispanics out of central cities meant that many have entered declining industrial suburbs. A striking example of the Hispanic experience occurred in Cicero, Illinois, a blue-collar suburb outside Chicago. It has long been lily-white and was the scene of racial violence in the mid-1960s when Martin Luther King attempted to effect black penetration. The 1980 census reported more than 5,000 Hispanics and only 74 blacks in Cicero, despite the fact that Hispanics made up only 12.5 percent of Chicago's population while blacks constituted over 33 percent.

Political Change

The concentration of blacks and Hispanics in urban areas, the civil rights movement, and recent legislation—especially the voting rights bill—have had significant political consequences. As in economic and employment changes for minorities, however, results have been far short of equal participation, but they have occasioned new patterns at all levels of government.

As recently as 1964, there were only 103 elected black officials throughout the nation. By July 1979, the number had increased to some 4,600, an impressive growth but still less than 1 percent of the total. In 1981, seventeen blacks and five Hispanics were members of the House of Representatives; many of the former, however, seemed temporarily threatened by projected redistricting as a consequence of the 1980 census. By 1979, over 190 towns and cities across the nation had elected black mayors; included were Los Angeles, Washington, Detroit, Atlanta, Cleveland, New Orleans, Oakland, Newark, and Gary. Since then, Birmingham and Richmond were added to the list. In 1981 San Antonio elected a Mexican-American mayor. It is, as might be expected, in municipal government that the interplay between ethnic groups has been most apparent.

A NEW ETHNIC TRANSITION AT CITY HALL

Black mayors have been elected in four of the five largest cities where blacks were a majority in 1980. Blacks were also a majority in five somewhat smaller cities; in four of these, there were black mayors. And in Cleveland and Los Angeles, when blacks were and still are less than a majority, other black mayors had been elected. Unless racial population movements depart from recent trends, it is highly probable that more of our cities will have black majorities and elect black mayors. By October 1981, it was clear that Hartford, Connecticut would soon be added to the list.

This potential gives rise to several questions. What does it imply for the economic future of the cities involved, and what role will white elites and white ethnics play in the process? Although it is too early to answer these questions with certainty, there is a rather careful analysis of two large cities with black mayors, both of whom had been reelected. Peter K. Eisinger's *The Politics of Displacement* probes into the issues delineated above and concentrates upon the groups which have lost power. His conviction is that the newly victorious group's ability to govern and the well-being of the cities will depend upon the response of the old white elite and teach us something about ethnic conflict and cooperation in the nation. This has great relevance to the subject of this chapter since white ethnic-minority competition has been recurrent and directed to varied aspects of American life, especially employment, education, and housing. It has also frequently been violent. In this setting, one might expect that the political "outs," having been reduced to minority status, might emulate a similar pattern of violence in a situation in which white ethnics and a racial minority are involved.

Eisinger also analyzes the new political coalitions which emerged in Detroit and Atlanta and the questions of whether or not federal support was endangered or state cooperation withdrawn. As is carefully pointed out, in several vital respects these two cities (which were the largest and smallest among the twenty-six most populous with black majorities) have similarities and differences, yet their experiences were strikingly parallel. Their mutual peculiarities, however, suggest that other large cities will not inevitably duplicate their responses.

The Transition in Boston—One of the earliest and perhaps the most dramatic ethnic transitions in municipal power was that which occurred in Boston at the close of the nineteenth and beginning of the twentieth century. The setting was one of extreme ethnic hostility filled with animosity, distrust, and disdain. So great were the differences between Yankee New England and the Irish, including the crucial one of religion, that genuine accommodation to the transition seemed impossible. Yet it did occur. Eisinger summarized the implications of this experience in one sentence. "The question that remains is whether the character of the transition in Boston was a product of New England genius or whether it illustrates a more general trait of adaptability in the American political system."

In the process of setting forth the Boston experience, he observes that violence between politically established and emerging political groups seems to occur principally in the earliest stages of the new group's mobilization and well in advance of the takeover. Mob violence against the Irish in Boston, for example, was concentrated between 1830 and 1850, several decades before the Irish had political visibility.

Black Political Ascendancy—One of the striking features about black political ascendance in Detroit and Atlanta was its inevitability. Race had been a pervasive element in the post-World War II politics of both cities. Until 1970 and thereafter, the white power elite in Atlanta had concentrated upon deflecting both black power and lower-class white racism, coopting the former and containing the latter. In the process, the white business elite developed lines of communication with leaders in the black community. In Detroit, black political development was dampened by the failure of the labor-led coalition (of which blacks were a part) to control its white ethnic rank and file. In both cities, black political participation was largely within perimeters established by white elites. As a result, blacks were kept out of the economic determination at city hall in Atlanta and long frustrated by being part of the losing coalition in Detroit. When that coalition did come to power, blacks did not achieve either influence in policy or significant political office. With the emergence of black majorities, blacks were able to break away from past white-dominated coalitions and became politically more independent. Their scope and influence on economic issues as well as access to policy determination and political office greatly increased.

In Atlanta, where there had been an almost indistinguishable identity between the white political and the economic elite, the latter was concerned and apprehensive about the transition and more than a bit nostalgic about "the good old days." Detroit was more realistic, and the white elite accepted the transition as inevitable, concentrating on how to live with it. Of course, the 1967 race riot had mellowed, frightened, and also educated them about the black community. Thus they recognized that the old days had not been so good. Whatever the differences and the apprehensions, the evidence seems to indicate that among the elites in both cities the assumption that black rule would be a durable phenomenon was a product of simple calculus. In Detroit, long exposure to white ethnic transitions softened the shock of having a black mayor. The apprehension in Atlanta was greater, but working with blacks on political issues was really not an innovation; the ground rules which would evolve were, however.

A New Political Coalition in Cities—One of the most significant features of the reign of blacks in city hall was the rise of a new coalition between black mayors and the white business structure. The first thing that strikes one about this is that both groups recognized its crucial importance for the survival of the city. It also symbolized the fact that in both locales the major economic actors did not contemplate abandonment of the city. From the point of view of the mayors, the coalition was essential because they needed the white elites who largely financed their campaigns, as well as supplied fiscal aid to the city. The newly elected mayors needed the black community which supplied the political power base that elected them. The white elites also provided a buffer against middle- and lower-class opposition from white ethnics in Detroit and the disorganized poor whites in Atlanta. From the point of view of the white elites, there were at least two principal benefits: the coalition enabled them to pursue their economic interests, supplying the necessary elements of city hall cooperation, and it tended to moderate the impact of the transition by putting a damper on rapid and radical social, economic, or political change.

Detroit and Atlanta demonstrated that black mayors, rather than being a detriment to securing federal assistance so vital to cities' survival, were actually an asset. This was, in part, due to the individuals who had been elected. Coleman Young was an early and ardent supporter of presidential candidate Carter, and Maynard Jackson had strong Georgia ties with Carter. Also, neither the state legislature of Michigan nor that of Georgia attempted to strip the power of the newly elected mayors, as did the state government of Massachusetts almost a century ago when the Irish ascended to political control in Boston. This was due, in no small measure, to the 9 percent of blacks in the Georgia State Assembly and Senate and the 10 percent of blacks in the Michigan legislature. Also, Georgia was proud of the image of its flagship city of Atlanta, and Detroit was equally symbolic of progress in Michigan.

The absence of organized and cohesive white opposition to black political control in Detroit was due to many circumstances. One was structural: the lack of a tradition and existence of political parties in municipal elections and the absence of the machine rule so often associated with strong ethnic organization and consciousness. For example, the resistance and actual sabotage of Mayor Richard Hatcher in Gary was triggered by white eastern European ethnics who controlled the city's political machine, and opposition to the accession of Wilson Frost, a black Chicago city councilman, to the position of acting mayor after Richard Daley's death was attributed to the machine which was fighting for survival. In contrast, the victories of Young and Jackson neither destroyed an effective party machine nor displaced a particular ethnic group or a coalition of such groups which had been in control of local government. Local observers described Detroit's ethnic groups, particularly those of European origin which not too long ago had spearheaded activity in the job and housing markets and had sabotaged Detroit's liberal-labor-black political coalition, as unorganized and lacking leadership. The structure of the city's political competition increasingly found expression in broad racial terms rather than as a matter of conflict between blacks and a particular white ethnic group. This led to a varied and diffuse reaction to the displacement within the widely diverse white ethnics. And, of course, it reduced the possibility of well-organized ethnic pressure to encourage and support elite resistance. As in most southern cities, the tradition of conflict in Atlanta was between whites and blacks across the board. Because of this and the composition of the population, the city had no self-conscious white ethnic groups of any consequence.

The coalition between black mayors and the white business elite is not without problems. One of the consequences of this collaboration was apparent benign neglect of the white middle class. This raises a question as to whether or not the coalition can continue to contain the opposition of the white middle class. An answer in the affirmative presents the issue of the price of white business support in terms of the goals of black political ascendancy.

It is unrealistic to expect that the coalition is capable of bringing about long-run basic changes needed to mount effective assaults on poverty, unemployment, ineffective public education, or inadequate housing. This follows from the lack of sufficient local resources to sustain most American cities, let alone deal with economic and social problems which are national in their scope and impact. It does not mean, however, that black mayors are powerless to ameliorate to some degree the deprivations of their constituents. Where there is a strong mayoral system of municipal government, takeover of city hall by blacks accelerates their constituents' protection against police brutality, sharing in public contracts, appointment to high echelon positions, expanded municipal employment, and improved public services. Efforts that would go further than provide incremental gains would alienate the white business interests which facilitated accommodation of black ascendancy in city hall. As Eisinger concluded:

> It is perhaps ironic, then, that the very achievement that has made possible the peaceful management of mature ethnic competition has also militated against the development of more novel and widespread

approaches to the solution of social and economic justice problems in urban America.

Nor is the prevalence or the nature of the transitional coalition a permanent one. This became evident in the 1981 mayoral primary contest in Atlanta when the coalition between the white power structure and the black candidate began to disintegrate.

Cities, Poverty, and Public Intervention

The American city traditionally provided a way station for the waves of immigrants who came from abroad, and by and large it ultimately treated them well. Most were not strangers to prejudice, slander, and hardship, including abominable housing in industrial centers, and unbelievable neglect of health and nutrition which led to extremely high morbidity and mortality rates. However, they learned the language, acquired new skills, and many went up the long tenement trail to relative affluence and acceptance into American society. But in recent decades, as minorities with varying degrees of black and Indian strains increasingly were involved, this historical role of the city has deteriorated badly. Its humanizing influence has faltered, and millions of recent black, Puerto Rican, and, to a slightly lesser degree, Mexican-Americans became trapped in racial ghettos. Once trapped, a large proportion of them are hard put to break away.

CITIES AND THE DISADVANTAGED

The problems of the urban disadvantaged and poor are problems of our cities. The problems of our cities are, in turn, in large part the problems of the disadvantaged and the poor. Economist Lester C. Thurow put the matter well when he wrote in 1977:

> The heart of the central city's economic problem is a long-run decline accelerated by a concentration of lower-income minority groups. . . . The problem of low minority incomes is not one of those problems that can be permanently buried. It can only be postponed temporarily since . . . [millions of] black Americans . . . and Spanish-origin Americans aren't going to go away. And until we solve this problem we are going to have a continually festering urban crisis.

In recent years two somewhat inconsistent phenomena have been and are occurring simultaneously. There has been an absolute and relative improvement in the economic status of well-trained blacks (and Mexican-Americans and Puerto Ricans), concurrent with a decline in the absolute and relative status of the unskilled, poorly trained, and inexperienced, as well as others who remain outside the mainstream of the economy. Median figures for income and unemployment fail to reveal this dichotomy. They understate somewhat the progress of the upwardly mobile while minimizing the relative deprivation of a sizable proportion of blacks and other minorities.

Since 1960, representation of blacks (for whom there are more data and analyses than for other minorities) in relatively high income managerial employment has increased. For those involved, the question in 1981 was whether or not they would gain admission to the highest rungs on the management ladder. According to an article in the *Wall Street Journal,* June 1981, there was more optimism than pessimism expressed by those on the way to the top. It must be realized, however, that this group and the rest of the black middle class are still a relatively small proportion. By 1977 only 9 percent of black families had incomes above the Bureau of Labor Statistics (BLS) level for a higher standard of living and only 24 percent above the BLS level for an intermediate standard of living. Comparable percentages for whites were 24 and 49 percent respectively.

Disastrously High Rates of Teenage Unemployment—As the living standards for privileged blacks eroded somewhat in the 1970s, the economic status of less affluent blacks has deteriorated much more rapidly. Youth have been the chief victims. Beginning in 1958, an increasing differential in unemployment rates between black and white youth developed. By 1970, in eleven central cities, it had become striking—at least twice as large for blacks in eight of them. Six years later unemployment for teenagers as a group had increased appreciably. For blacks the growth was dramatic, ranging in seven of the eleven cities from 42 to 58 percent. White youth unemployment in these same cities ranged from 12 to 25 percent. A 1980 Department of Labor study reported "unemployment among youths in general and among youths from minority groups in particular, already recognized as a major social and economic problem, is even more severe than generally believed." Nor is the situation peculiar to blacks. Census estimates for 1979 reported unemployment among 34 percent of male black youth, 23 percent for young Hispanic males, and 16 percent for young white males. In chapter 4 Professor Cafferty presents data indicating that the rate of unemployment among mainland urban male Puerto Rican youth was more than double that for urban male Mexican-American youth in 1976.

The Poverty Trap and Its Consequences for Cities—These and other data and studies repudiate the notion that minorities are rapidly moving into the mainstream of national economic life as did earlier arrivals to the cities. A growing number of minority families are below the official poverty level, and millions in the ghettos are parts of families which for three or more generations have been in the poverty trap. Sociologists speak of this situation in terms of "The City As Sandbox," "The City As Reservation," or more recently, "The Central Cities As Storage Bins for People Who Have No Productive Roles in the Market Economy." Continuing poverty among minorities, especially among the youth, amidst general affluence is a threat to our economic, social, and political system. Youth and many others who share their poverty, joblessness, and lack of legitimate opportunities are prone to enter the street life of hustling. Alienated from society, they have little or no vested interest in it or its economic and social institutions. Events in England in the summer of 1981 dramatically demonstrated this.

INCOME TRANSFER PROGRAMS AS ALTERNATIVE
SOURCES OF LIVELIHOOD

Income transfer programs serve two purposes. They have become a significant component in the package of federal fiscal assistance to the cities. At the same time, they are a vital instrument for alleviating the human costs of poverty in a society of general well-being. If the fiscal woes of the cities were not so heavily involved with human problems, there would be no rationale for the use of income transfer programs as a mechanism for providing financial aid to cities. Indeed, direct grants either as general revenue sharing or for categorical uses, such as upgrading infrastructure, would be a more effective and economical instrument. But pockets of poverty are both a financial burden and a social threat to many cities.

A second point is that income transfer programs targeted at those capable of working were conceived as a temporary source of livelihood. A corollary to this was and remains development and support of programs which will expand the volume of jobs, train effectively the unemployed to qualify for work, and take steps to assure their access to the expanded employment. If these steps are taken—and we have not done so to date—it is possible to design income transfer programs so as to minimize the recipients' withdrawal from the labor force. On the other hand, to design these programs so as to discourage other than short-time dependence upon them and also fail to provide expanding job opportunities brings extreme deprivation and dilutes the efforts' amelioration of widespread hostility.

Even in periods of high unemployment, many who receive income transfer payments are too old or too young to work, are handicapped, or suffer from other physical or mental disabilities which prevent their full-time employment. A large number are women with small children. For such clients, structural changes in, and more expert administration of, the programs would render them less costly and more effective. Obviously these reforms should be encouraged. But the problems which income transfer programs address will remain and cry out for recognition and reform in a humane society.

LIMITATIONS OF THE MARKET

Market forces, even in unique periods of extreme labor shortage when they serve ultimately to expand the volume of minority employment, have provided only limited upward mobility for racial minorities in this country. The road to occupational upgrading for these groups has been one of agitation, legislation, and litigation engendered primarily by blacks. Each of the major minorities has expanded its economic opportunities, in large measure, through public service. This has been especially true for white-collar, management, and professional work. The earlier small black middle class, for example, had as its backbone government workers, especially teachers, post office employees, a few clerks, and a larger number of messengers. Only the latter three, however, were outside the physical and social confines of the ghetto; preachers and teachers, like the much lesser number of doctors, dentists, lawyers, and morticians, were a part of a segregated society and economy.

Minority groups in America owe what economic progress they have made primarily to two circumstances: to situations of labor shortage, notably occasioned by wars or war preparation, and to public intervention. Without the latter, the market, even at times of labor shortage, has been slow in affording them greatly expanded employment opportunities and ineffectual in providing access to high echelon jobs. This was dramatically illustrated in World War II.

To appreciate the limitations of the market in reducing discrimination and accelerating equal job opportunity, it is necessary to recognize the contrast between free enterprisers' concept of a competitive market and reality. As Anderson and Cottingham observed, were there free competition and were all parties beginning with comparable assets and enjoying comparable bargaining power in the labor market, the free play of that market might operate to minimize discrimination. But in actuality, such conditions do not exist; thus there is need for public intervention to supplement and often modify the impact of the market. It is vital to recognize this at a time when we are advised to depend upon rising economic tides to lift all the boats. The rising tide does little or nothing to help ships wrecked at the bottom of the sea.

The Importance of Public Intervention—In the last half of the twentieth century government took a significant lead role in the upward occupational mobility of minorities. As early as the New Deal and extending into the defense program, the federal government began to provide an increase in white-collar and a few professional jobs for blacks. In areas where minorities were able to vote, state and local governments followed suit. As the somewhat expanded new minority middle class came into being in the 1960s and subsequently, public service again played a major role. At all levels of government, it provided new and higher levels of professional and managerial jobs to minorities, while greatly expanding white-collar opportunities, particularly at the clerical level.

Government's impact did not stop in-house. In many occupations it led the way to expanded private employment. This involved three activities.

1. Setting an example and providing access to experience. An instance of what was involved is found in the legal profession. Government appointment of blacks as agency attorneys, prosecuting attorneys, attorneys general and their associates and assistants, and as judges in superior court generally preceded the recruitment of blacks by the large private law firms and large corporations (a process which is still in its infancy). Also the appointment of blacks to the Federal Reserve Board and the Import-Export Bank was not unrelated to blacks' subsequent, hesitant, but continuing utilization as professionals by Wall Street, banking, insurance, and related financial institutions. Indeed when President Lyndon Johnson designated Andrew F. Brimmer as the first black governor of the Federal Reserve Board, he told the present writer that one of the reasons for doing so was to accelerate acceptance of black professionals by the private financial institutions.
2. Prohibiting racial discrimination in employment first in public service and then in private firms with defense and other public contracts.
3. Requiring affirmative action to achieve equal employment opportunity.

Few members of minority groups are unaware of the difference public intervention has made in their economic status. Of course, they are equally conscious of its role in securing their access to public facilities, protection against violence, and the right to vote.

The access of minorities to the suburbs, too, is in part a response to public intervention. Although there are grave deficiencies in the enforcement machinery in Title VIII of the Civil Rights Act of 1968 which outlaws racial discrimination in housing, it has served to widen minorities' access to shelter. For the market to be an effective instrument to provide equal employment or shelter opportunities it must be free and competitive. To assume that it is, in a situation of widespread de facto residential segregation, is to assure the perpetuation of such market-approved discrimination.

AFFIRMATIVE ACTION

The earlier emphasis upon the peculiar persistence and unique intensity of past and current discrimination against minorities is pertinent to an understanding of their current status and an evaluation of actions taken to improve it. This analysis is no less relevant to the debate about the relative significance of race versus class in deterring or accelerating the upward mobility of minorities.

Recently there has been recognition that both race and class are involved in analyzing the present status of blacks. Those who accentuate the importance of class, however, ignore the fact that race has been a primary factor in creating the economic, social, educational, and political experiences which have had so great a role in affecting the upward mobility of blacks, and thereby dictating their class. As Thomas F. Pettigrew of Harvard recently observed in *Daedalus,* "Race and social class increasingly interact to produce critical effects that cannot be explained by simply combining the main effects of the two factors."

It is in recognition of the complexities of economic discrimination that public policy has evolved from nondiscrimination to equal opportunity and to affirmative action. Affirmative action is an unabashed administrative remedy designed to correct past discrimination or ameliorate its effects. Basically, affirmative action involves setting numerical goals and timetables for the employment of minorities and women. At a time when racial discrimination increasingly is becoming more subtle in response to equal opportunity legislation, effective public intervention calls for objective criteria for compliance. The burning issue for many is imposition of quotas. As one who has spent the better part of a professional life spanning fifty years attempting to translate nondiscrimination policy into equal opportunity practices, I am convinced of the necessity for quantitative goals, especially in employment. There is, however, some room for varying formulas in different job classifications, for reasonably flexible timetables, and for using training and upgrading to achieve significant results.

Former Secretary of Transportation William T. Coleman, a black who is never hesitant to assert his Republicanism, put the case for affirmative action succinctly in his June 11, 1981, testimony before the Subcommittee on Constitutional Rights of the Senate Judiciary Committee.

> The consequences of centuries of slavery and second-class citizenship cannot be overcome by simply pretending that those consequences do not exist. It is nothing but a sham to allocate jobs, university admissions,

government contracts, and other scarce opportunities and resources on the basis of so-called "neutral" criteria that in fact perpetuate the legacy of slavery and discrimination. Bringing real equality into the mainstream of American culture and purging that culture of the effects of racism and racial segregation will take many more decades of committed effort.

Impact of Ethnicity

WHITE ETHNICS

In reacting to minority issues, white ethnics are really expressing their Americanism. They often do so in a peculiarly intense manner, particularly when they have become proponents of ethnicity. This is due to several circumstances.

1. They remain in close proximity to minorities in the labor market and temporally in terms of their relatively recent economic status.
2. For basically the same reasons as other whites, many resist residential integration and school desegregation; in addition, those who embrace ethnicity often rationalize espousal of neighborhood preservation and integrity long after these attributes have been substantially lost or significantly diluted, thereby bringing even greater emotional involvement.
3. In spite of their relative upward mobility, rivalry between them and minorities, often manipulated and orchestrated by dominant economic forces and institutions, has deep historical roots. In a period of recession and high levels of unemployment, this rivalry again seems a real or potential threat. It is an issue around which ethnics can quickly coalesce.
4. As minority groups move up into professional and managerial jobs, they become competitors (and often threats) to white ethnics. Some involved were formerly among minorities' staunchest allies, largely on the basis of liberal ideology. Those among them who have deserted or diluted their earlier liberal stance often become neoconservatives.
5. White ethnicity, stressing as it usually does the group's intrinsic talents, traditions, and culture, has significant impact upon intergroup relations in cities. This follows from these ethnic groups' minimizing the structural elements that have such great influence on the economic status and mobility of all those who enter industry at the bottom.

In short, viewing minorities from their own relative success in overcoming extreme hardship, white ethnics like neoconservatives greatly exaggerate the upward mobility society affords minorities and the progress of the latter in entering the mainstream of

America. Proponents of white ethnicity feel that because their ancestors and they "made it" without public intervention in general, and without affirmative action in particular, the more recent urban newcomers could and should do so also. They fail to comprehend that the economy their ancestors entered was quite different in its capacity to utilize unskilled labor from that of today, and they seem incapable of differentiating between the extreme initial racism and the hostility their ancestors encountered and the deep-seated racism that still haunts blacks and some other minorities. Nor do they recognize that residential segregation of black Americans, Puerto Ricans, and often Chicanos is quite different from that of Irish Catholics, Polish-Americans, Italian-Americans, Jews, or even WASPs. It is a great deal less voluntary and a great deal more pervasive. It is much less related to pluralism than enforced separatism.

Like the Reagan administration, many forget that even if the economic policies of supply economics work, an uncertain eventuality at best and an unlikely assumption at worst, it will take time for its benefits to trickle down to the hard-core unemployed. When and if they do, only a small sector of those at the bottom will rise, and the deprivation of the poor will become more pronounced. Proponents of white ethnicity have been slow to realize that in most instances the social programs identified for cutbacks by the present administration serve people in need and, at least over the short run, provide hope and assistance if not redemption. As noted earlier, these programs are not only people-oriented but the federal funds involved are a vital part of cities' budgets. By insensitivity to these issues, white ethnicity accentuates the economic crisis facing so many cities.

MINORITIES

The realities of the 1960s led to repudiation of the melting pot concept on the part of an impressive number of minority intellectuals. Some of this new breed of black, Mexican-American, and Puerto Rican writers borrowed concepts from the experiences of the former European colonies. While there were many striking parallels, there were also impressive deviations often minimized in an effort to establish the analogy. But the new model went far in challenging and discrediting the ethnic-assimilationist approach. It also was compatible with earlier espousal of a cultural-nationalist emphasis.

Ethnicity among minorities, for all it does to compensate for their having been deprived of their history in many brutal ways and as much as it may do for their ego status, serves to impede coalitions among them and with others. Also, it delays effective action to deal with urban problems, since some in minority groups fail to face up to the fact that their fate is inextricably linked both to the industrial world and to American cities. As noted above, it is, in large measure, a reaction to continuing and pervasive discrimination and rejection. As such, it discourages self-analysis. Almost two decades ago, I observed that the tragedy of discrimination was that it is a barrier to success and an excuse for failure. Ethnicity, too, can inhibit realistic evaluation of the possibility of dealing effectively with the needs of the urban underclass within the structure of minority ghettos. It can also be a factor leading to undue optimism about the impact of enterprise zones as a basic element in the economic salvation of minorities.

The stakes are high. Unless the problems of our urban areas are addressed and resolved, the nation's economic, social, and political health is threatened. There is the possibility of inter-group conflict and the long-run potential of "The City As Reservation." This becomes even more ominous as the wave of political conservatism sweeps the country and benign neglect of the disadvantaged passes from rhetoric to public policy.

Pastora San Juan Cafferty

4

The Language Question:

The Dilemma of Bilingual Education for Hispanics in America

Introduction

Educational policy, crafted with the express intent of transmitting knowledge, perhaps reflects cultural values more than policies in other areas. Education was one of the earliest social services provided in American communities, and educational policy and programs date back to colonial times. Very early in its history, the American nation recognized the importance of education as a means of teaching succeeding generations of immigrants American norms and values. The young states funded public education, required knowledge of the English language, and demanded a degree of literacy as a condition of suffrage. Public support of educational programs was urged so that the children of immigrants would be socialized into the emerging American culture. The popular *New England Primer* and *Mc-*

PASTORA SAN JUAN CAFFERTY *is an associate professor at the School of Social Service Administration at the University of Chicago and a research associate at the National Opinion Research Center. Dr. Cafferty serves on many committees and boards of directors, including the Kimberly-Clark Corporation. She has written numerous articles and books, the most recent being* The Politics of Language: The Dilemma of Bilingual Education for Puerto Ricans.

Guffey's Reader imparted lessons in morals and politics as well as English language skills.

For the past two centuries, educational policy and the public school system have been seen as key components in bringing about social change. It was a public school education that distinguished the American native from his immigrant parents and provided him with the opportunity for economic and social advancement. Equality of education was seen as a prerequisite to equality of opportunity.

It is in this context that one must address the issue of bilingualism among the Hispanics in contemporary American society. There is good reason for the fact that any discussion of bilingualism immediately becomes a discussion of bilingual education: the mastering of a language and the understanding and appreciation of a culture always involve a process of learning. It is also important to note that the history of organized language consciousness, language loyalty, and language maintenance by different groups is a political history; it is the history of the formation of the large nation states. The struggle for linguistic dominance is closely allied to the struggle for political and economic dominance among differing ethnic groups.

This may be why bilingualism—more specifically, the issue of bilingual education—is the issue most often discussed when one discusses Hispanics in American society. The demand for bilingual education by the Hispanics is rightly seen as a socio-economic political issue.

THE QUESTION TO BE ADDRESSED

Before the complexity of the phenomena of bilingualism among the Hispanics in America can be addressed, one must ask whether bilingualism should be encouraged in the United States as a matter of policy for any or all ethnic groups—that is to say, whether institutions should exist which foster bilingualism and whether these institutions should be supported not only by the ethnic group but by majority society. In order to answer this question one must first look to the reality of the history of the American nation of immigrants and then to the Hispanic immigration experience in the context of that history.

Bilingual Individuals—If bilingualism is to be encouraged, then one must ask whether it is the individual who is to be bilingual or the nation. American society is strongly monolingual. There are historical and economic as well as political reasons for this, and there is no evidence that it is changing. Indeed, there is some evidence that while there is strong native language retention among a number of ethnic groups, there is no greater incidence of this retention than there was at the beginning of the century.

Indeed, there is decreasing incidence of native language retention among Hispanics. This fact is often ignored because of two reasons: there has always been greater native language retention among Hispanics than among other immigrant groups, and the number of Hispanics *in proportion* to the rest of the United States population is continually increasing. Their number grew from between 9 to 12 million in 1970 to 14.6 million in 1980, according to preliminary census figures. This does not include the 3 million Hispanics in Puerto Rico. Many demographers predict that Hispanics will be the largest minority in American society by the end of the century; many sociologists and educators are concerned they will constitute a large *linguistic* minority.

In spite of this concern, there should be little serious risk that America will become a bilingual nation. The language of the marketplace both here and abroad will continue to be English. The American economy continues to demand English-language skills of those who wish to participate in it. The majority of immigrants came to America for economic reasons and will learn English in order to participate in its economic benefits. The question is not whether America will become a bilingual society; the question becomes whether society should encourage the existence and maintenance of bilingualism in the individual.

Bilingual Institutions—The next question to be answered is whether society should support bilingual institutions. If American society is English dominant, should it create bilingual institutions to serve the needs of those who do not speak English? If so, should these institutions be for everyone? Should they be everywhere? If not, for whom and where should they exist? These questions are not unrelated to the first: if individuals are truly bilingual, they will need a minimum of bilingual institutions. However, there is at minimum a period of transition when the individual functions best—if not exclusively—using his native language.

The question of provision of bilingual services ranges from providing signs in English and Spanish in public transit in Chicago to funding bilingual programs in public schools. Churches and social service agencies have traditionally offered services in the native language to immigrant communities. The history of parochial school education in America was often a history of bilingual education. Society has always recognized that individuals are best served in the language which they know best. The question is simply whether American society as a matter of public policy should foster bilingual institutions.

Two Monolingual Cultures—Perhaps the most important—and the most often spoken—question is whether American society should encourage bilingualism in the sense of two monolingual cultures. This could occur where there is a high enough density of Hispanics—in certain areas of the Southwest, of the Northeast, or in South Florida. The fact is that such monolingual communities exist. They are often socioeconomic as well as linguistic ghettos. If anything will prevent their growth, it may be the creation of bilingual individuals who will span the cultural differences between the majority and minority communities.

THE ISSUE OF BILINGUAL EDUCATION

Bilingual education may be defined as transitional or maintenance. Transitional education is designed to provide a temporary bridge to the majority language. Maintenance education is designed to enhance and maintain the student's language and culture while teaching the second language and transmitting the values and culture of the host country.

Language and Culture

Language as a means of preserving culture is the history of every society. The history of organized language consciousness, language loyalty, and language maintenance by different ethnic groups in the Western world dates back more than five centuries to the formation of the large nation states and the colonization of the New World.

In the New World, the preservation of native languages by the indigenous inhabitants of South American countries reflects the preservation of indigenous culture. In countries such as Ecuador and Peru, where the native culture plays a vital contemporary role, particularly in the remote mountain areas, the indigenous languages are preserved, sometimes to the exclusion of the national language, Spanish. Those who have kept their native language live in isolation from the Spanish-speaking majority. This isolation, partly a result of the inaccessibility of the mountain areas, results in preservation of a society which is markedly different from that of the country as a whole. In this case, the preservation of the indigenous language and culture is not a conscious assertion of ethnic identity but the result of little or no exposure to the host culture. In Canada a long history of linguistic division which reflects the political and cultural division between the French and English Canadians is reflected in the conscious assertion of monolingual French- and English-speaking societies which have struggled for dominance and achieved an uneasy coexistence in the bilingual nation. It was largely the fear of political division and domestic dissension which gave impetus to monolingualism in America. The European experience had provided the young nation with ample evidence that language was a powerful force in establishing and maintaining national loyalty.

LINGUISTIC ASSIMILATION

The flood of immigrants pouring into the new nation after 1776 led to the developing Anglo-Saxon race consciousness and to a distinction between those who had migrated before 1776 and the immigrants who came shortly after. Those who migrated before 1776 were dubbed "colonists" and were praised as brave idealists who migrated for religious and political freedom; the more recent "immigrants" were accused of coming to America only to benefit from the material prosperity the New World offered. Patriotic societies which excluded the new immigrants were founded at this time by the colonists.

Europeans had from earliest days migrated to America for a

variety of reasons. A few had come seeking religious and political freedom; the majority had come seeking economic opportunity—particularly the privilege of owning land. Even those who sailed on the *Mayflower* numbered among them skilled laborers who were not of the Puritan faith. However, the mythology which idealizes the older immigrants at the expense of more recent arrivals is one that has shaped attitudes toward immigration throughout American history. Early in the colonial period, voices were raised in protest against some of the non-English elements that entered the colonies. The Scotch-Irish were viewed as a problem by the Quakers in Pennsylvania who found them to be aggressive and lawless. As early as 1729, a Pennsylvania statute sought to protect the colony against those likely to become public charges and to penalize those who brought in such elements.

Very early in American history, the English-speaking were identified as the most desirable settlers. The colonies had been settled under the protection of the British Crown; the wealthy merchants who traded with the mother country, the holders of large tracts of land from the King, and the political rulers were all English-speaking. The powerful and wealthy spoke English. Nearly two centuries of British rule imprinted the British language and culture as that of the majority society.

The English-speaking assimilated easily into the society of the British colonies. Immigrants who did not speak English soon discovered the desirability of learning the new language. To speak English was proof of one's acceptance of American culture and values and of one's assimilation into American society. It was also desirable for economic and social mobility. The new immigrant had to learn English to communicate with his employer, to transact business, and to understand the laws. A common language was necessary for all settlers in the colonies to communicate with each other. It was only logical that the language should be the English language of the mother country.

Strains of ethnocentrism and nativism at different periods in American history reflected derision and fear of "foreign" languages and "foreign" accents. Immigrants unable to speak and write English were classified as "illiterate" and, often, as "ignorant" and were subjected to social and economic sanctions. Employers often advertised for "English-speaking" workers in eighteenth-century broadsides. Papers and etiquette books published in the early nineteenth century stressed the importance of speaking English correctly in order to be accepted in polite society.

The Importance of Linguistic Assimilation—Societies view linguistic change as one of the prime targets for breaking down old loyalties and adapting to a new culture. The reverse is also true: the retention of the native language provides an effective shield against assimilation. The right most often sought by groups who are struggling to maintain their ethnic identity in the face of assimilation into the dominant society is the provision of adequate education in the group's own tongue as well as the recognition of the group's language as an official government language. It is not surprising, then, that a society which stressed the assimilation of immigrants would demand linguistic assimilation as well.

Speaking a common language was important to forging a common national identity. Benjamin Franklin's concern that the members of the Pennsylvania legislature would be unable to communicate with one another because half would speak English and the other half speak German was evidence of a realistic concern. If different language groups were allowed to preserve their native languages to the exclusion of English, political dissension was a serious possibility. German farmers who did not see the colonists' quarrel with England as their own came close to rebellion in Pennsylvania following the end of the Revolutionary War. It was important for the immigrants to have as much in common as possible in order to create a national identity: a common language was essential to achieve this.

The policy of English monolingualism in America has been justified for almost 200 years on the assumption that immigrants to America, who come to stay in a land promising political and religious freedom, will become citizens and that their children will become a new generation of native Americans. While some immigrants did return, the majority of the immigrants came to stay. Early pamphlets and tracts extolling the virtues of migration to America were circulated throughout Europe. They all stressed the permanence of the migration. Indeed the journey was long and expensive. Most immigrants came with little hope of return.

Return Migration—It is futile to argue what complex motives led millions of immigrants to leave home and risk the rigors of an ocean crossing, but from the beginning many came to find work. And many of these who did find work returned home with their earnings. As early as 1860, there are reports of workers from Lancashire, iron molders from Scotland, and coal miners from other parts of the United Kingdom returning home. Some immigrants tended to return more than others: for the most part the Irish stayed, while hundreds of thousands of British workers came and went reflecting economic cycles. Although there were few studies of return migration in America, the data available support the fact that return migration was always a major factor in American migration. There has always been a pattern of immigration and emigration, for every major stream a counter-stream developed. For the most part, the returning immigrant has been ignored. This is unfortunate since the fine studies that do exist seem to indicate that the decision to return or to stay is directly related to the degree in which the immigrant adapts to American society.

FOREIGN LANGUAGE SCHOOLS

While many American immigrants did return, the majority stayed. Among those groups who tended to remain were the Germans, and it is among the Germans that the greatest efforts were made to retain native language and culture. Theirs is the oldest and most persistent immigrant language community in the United States, beginning in 1683 in Pennsylvania and still maintaining a vigorous dialect. As early as 1694, there were schools which taught German language near Philadelphia. Bilingual instruction in German and English was introduced at the University of Pennsylvania in 1780 and several years later at Franklin College in Lancaster. Before 1800, the Germans had parochial schools throughout the country.

Bilingual Education in Religious Schools—Other immigrants organized efforts at preserving language and culture around the church and parochial schools. Notable among these were the Czechs and Slovaks who, in addition to parochial schools, supported language schools after school hours and on weekends. In addition, many Czechs went to German language schools where they found similar customs and religious instruction. However,

Czech parishes had their own language schools well into the twentieth century. The break with Catholicism sent many Czechs to public schools where the process of Americanization was completed.

The French in New England and the Scandinavians and Dutch in the Midwest had their schools. While some of these were monolingual schools, the majority offered bilingual education. After 1800, the Germans, French, and Scandinavians continued to operate parochial schools as did the new immigrants, particularly the Poles, Lithuanians, and Slovaks. The effort to preserve language by immigrants in America is closely aligned to efforts to preserve religious belief and provides the evidence that language is seen as the catalyst to preserving cultural values. However, not all language preservation efforts were church related.

Bilingual Education in the Public Schools—Between 1840 and 1880, bilingual programs were offered in the public schools. In addition to German bilingual education, there were French-English schools in Louisiana and Spanish-English schools in New Mexico. After 1880, only one group successfully maintained bilingual programs in the public schools—the Germans, who did so until 1917.

There is no evidence that bilingual programs were welcomed by the community at large. Rather, there is substantial evidence to show that efforts at maintaining a bilingual community were always resisted in America. Bilingual programs existed in the public schools due to the political pressure exerted by ethnic communities; they were merely tolerated by the English-speaking. The bilingual programs were language programs offering little challenge to the melting pot theory of cultural assimilation.

The experience of the Germans in Cincinnati illustrates this. The Germans, who believed the American public schools to be inferior to those they had left in Germany, founded their own German-language parochial schools in Ohio. In 1840, bilingual education was instituted in the public schools of Ohio not to encourage linguistic and cultural pluralism but to ensure that German children would also learn English. The Germans wanted their own schools to retain their ethnic identity; the state was willing to fund such schools to effect assimilation. Although German language programs continued until World War II, not one single community maintained a language program adequately supported by the population it served that lasted over any extended period of time. The evidence suggests that bilingual public schools aided the process of assimilation.

Bilingual Education Efforts Cease—Following World War I, all efforts at bilingual education—education in and through the native language—ceased in public schools in the United States, although certain parishes continued to teach the native language in parochial and Sunday schools. The United States, having fought a war to save democracy and end all future wars, had emerged as a major world power. Americans asserted the uniqueness of their democratic experience and of all things American, including the American language. The political rhetoric, as well as the press and radio, denounced all things foreign and praised all things American. The European experience was described as decayed and corrupt, and those who had come to America were exhorted to cast off the old man of Europe and become the new American man. Consequently, there was little interest in foreign languages during the decades of the twenties, thirties, and forties. After 1945, foreign language efforts were focused on teaching English as a second language—efforts to assimilate the immigrants who continued to cling stubbornly to their native tongues.

THE RETENTION OF NATIVE LANGUAGE

In spite of this, each group of immigrants, with varying amounts of success, has attempted to preserve its culture by preserving linguistic identity. The success of these efforts is dramatic proof of the immigrants' need to preserve their native culture while becoming part of the new American society.

Language Retention Among the Europeans—The Germans, who have the longest and most persistent history of bilingual education in America, also are among those who assimilated most successfully. They insisted on preserving their language and culture for generations through the establishment and support of parochial and private German language schools. They even succeeded at certain times in establishing publicly funded bilingual education. Undoubtedly, each subsequent stream of German migration contributed to these efforts. However, each group assimilated into the economic mainstream of America.

Other immigrant groups struggled less successfully to preserve their native tongue and ways while becoming Americans. The success of these efforts is shown by the fact that in 1971, the Center for Applied Linguistics estimated 20 million Americans had a non-English native tongue. During the hearings on the Bilingual Education Act of 1968, representatives from the U.S. Office of Education testified that more than 3 million American children still spoke a language other than English. Of these, 1.75 million spoke Spanish; the remainder spoke some thirty other languages, including French, Italian, Polish, German, and Czech.

Language Retention Among the Spanish-Speaking—It is the Spanish-speaking who, as a people, have had the greatest retention of native language in the United States. In the case of the Mexican-American in the Southwest, retention of Spanish language and culture can be attributed to a proximity to Mexico and to the continuing stream of Mexican migrant workers, as well as to isolation and exclusion by the English-speaking society. The native Spanish language has been preserved for two centuries by the descendants of the Mexicans who inhabited the Southwest territories annexed after the War of 1848. There is evidence that the preservation of native language and culture in America is greatest in rural areas where migrants were isolated and continued to communicate in their native tongue. This may account for initial retention of Spanish language and culture in the Southwest. Another factor may be that the retention of Spanish language and culture was guaranteed to the people of the Southwest under the Treaty of Guadalupe Hidalgo.

However, Spanish-language retention continues among the increasingly urban Spanish-speaking population in contemporary America. Proximity and the phenomenon of cyclical migration may be the two factors that most contribute to the continuing preservation of Spanish as a native language among the nation's 14 million Hispanics.

The Dynamics of Immigration

In order to understand the Hispanic migration, one must study it in the context of the history of all migrations in the United States. American immigration history has focused largely on the Europeans who traveled to make their homes in the new land. Since this European migration was a major factor in the creation of the American nation, it has become the stuff of which myths are made. The fact is that most Europeans, like Hispanics, came seeking jobs and not all Europeans came to stay. It is also a fact that the migration from Europe has always been accompanied by a large-scale internal migration in which a majority of American citizens participate.

If not all immigrants who came to America stayed, at least cost and distance made the decision to return as seemingly irrevocable as the initial decision to migrate. The man who left his village to walk to the unknown cities of his country and then continue the far-away journey to seaports as exotic to him as a foreign land made a series of decisions on the way to America which made his migration a carefully considered act. Poverty and hunger may have pushed him away from home and the fields generations of his family had tilled; the lure of untold riches and tales of owning pasture and farmland that reached as far as the eye could see may have pulled him to the promise of America. But the decision was difficult. The journey across the sea was hard. Storms and disease claimed lives. The diet of hardtack and fetid water weakened the immigrant who, if he were among the lucky ones, would land in New York a pale and worn man very different from the suntanned peasant who had left the village many months before.

The journey did not become easier with the invention of the steamship which plied the ocean making frequent and regular trips between the East Coast cities and the teeming European harbors. Although the journey may have become more certain, it was not more pleasant. Immigrants were crowded into small and windowless cabins to cross an ocean that was just as unknown and, thus, just as fearful. Fear of the unknown has always given rise to strange fantasies.

CANADIANS, MEXICANS, AND PUERTO RICANS

The poor and unskilled from all nations traveled to America seeking jobs. However, in the case of Canadians, Mexicans, and Puerto Ricans the trip was short. They came from rural societies and saw opportunities for advancement in the United States that they believed could not be achieved in their own lands. Like the majority of European immigrants, their desire to migrate was based on the economic advantages to be gained. Both the Canadians and the Mexicans could, and did, walk to their new home—and their new jobs. Some might have traveled by horse and wagon—later in a bus or truck—but proximity was a key factor in the decision to migrate, a factor which did not diminish in importance throughout the migration experience. Puerto Ricans began traveling by ship to New York in the nineteenth century. Following World War II, they could make the six-hour trip for the price of a thirty-five dollar plane ticket. Thousands saved and borrowed to come to work in the North; others had recruiters from farms in New Jersey and Connecticut gladly pay the air fare to guarantee cheap labor to harvest the crops.

For all three groups, the migration patterns form a rather steady stream to the same communities throughout the nation. Interestingly, the patterns have varied little during the twentieth century, suggesting that both the promise of jobs and the comfort of joining relatives and friends in an unknown land are repeated from one generation to the next. In all groups, migration by whole families occurred; a family network was established so that family members were key sources of information. Family members who migrated first aided others in finding jobs and homes.

All three groups have resisted a permanent migration. The ease of travel facilitates migration so that an individual can come to the United States at no great financial or psychological costs. All three groups have been largely rural. All, as groups, have been relatively homogeneous. Almost all have come as skilled or semiskilled labor. This suggests that the rural to urban migration is more than a simple process of leaving the farm in the homeland to travel to a city in the United States. Rather, the migrant first leaves his farm to find work in a city in his homeland and then travels on, seeking a better job with better pay in the United States.

SPANISH-SPEAKING MIGRANTS

While there is little national concern about the hundreds of thousands of Canadians who migrate to the United States, there is grave concern about a closely parallel Mexican migration. The two migration streams are similar: (1) both have resisted assimilation and maintained close ties to the homeland; (2) both fled poor economic conditions and were drawn to economic opportunities here; and (3) both have remained in large numbers, but those who have remained have retained their ties with their families and homelands. Given similar circumstances, the immigrant from Canada blends in to such a degree that his existence is largely ignored. However, the Mexican immigrant with his darker skin and Spanish language is more visible.

The Mexican Immigrant—Mexicans constitute the largest immigration stream among the Hispanics. While legal immigration from Mexico numbers in the thousands annually, illegal immigration is impossible to measure. Estimates range from 2 to 10 million. Studies show that whatever the numbers, it is largely a circular migration. The illegal immigrant—like his legal counterpart—makes frequent extended visits to his homeland.

The Puerto Rican Migrant—The Puerto Ricans are part of the same constant stream of internal migration in America. They are citizens of the United States, traveling within its national boundaries. Yet, along with the other Hispanics, they are seen as foreigners, who take jobs and housing away from Americans on the mainland.

Other Hispanic Immigrants—Not enough is known about other Hispanic immigrants. The Cubans constituted a refugee migration which was initially welcomed. In the early 1960s when the American economy was strong and Americans accepted a commitment to receive those fleeing Communist rule, the federal government instituted a number of direct service programs to aid the Cubans. Many states and municipalities followed suit. Cubans clustered in southern Florida and northern New Jersey and were accepted by the majority society as a hard-working immigrant population which shared American middle-class values. In the 1980s, Cuban refugees, expelled by Castro, were not as readily welcomed by either majority society nor by other Cubans who had preceded them. In fact, Cubans had, since the early sixties, exhibited all the assimilation difficulties of any other refugee group. Traditionally refugees have not done as well economically as economic immigrants. An interesting study for the U.S. Department of Labor showed that Cubans had not done as well as Mexican immigrants who had comparable educational achievement. Of course the majority of the initial wave of Cuban refugees were highly educated.

Very little is known about the newest groups of Hispanic immigrants from Central and South America and the Caribbean. Many of them constitute part of the large illegal immigration stream. If they behave like the Mexicans and Canadians, they will also be circular migrants.

In his now classic study on Puerto Ricans, sociologist C. Wright Mills concluded that the most important factor in adaptation is language proficiency. The importance of language identity in the Mills study is basically confirmed by Joshua Fishman's study of bilingualism in the *barrio*. A series of interviews with leaders in the Puerto Rican community revealed the importance they placed on speaking Spanish in identifying themselves as Puerto Rican. Fishman goes so far as to maintain that "the Spanish language is the major link that unites intellectual and common Puerto Ricans in New York."

This is not surprising and may be more complex than it appears. For the insistence on speaking Spanish and the rejection of English may be a conscious affirmation of cultural retention. However, language proficiency is but one test of cultural assimilation. Since language is the articulation of a culture, the fact that Hispanics continue to speak Spanish may be evidence of their retention of their culture. The ease of travel is a major factor in return migration. The almost rhythmic ebb and flow of migration from Latin American countries to the United States continues to strengthen the Hispanics' retention of their native culture which, in turn, delays assimilation. As is the case with other migrants, Hispanics wish to return home. The difference is that many of them do. For those who return, the experience of having lived in the United States may indeed prove to be economically beneficial. Many return as highly skilled laborers.

The Rationale for Bilingual Education Policy

Language and cultural conflict may account for a good part of the Hispanic immigrants' problems. Resolution of these problems is thus closely tied to the mitigation of the conflict. Before one can address the conflict—and propose policies and programs

—one must determine how Hispanic immigrants differ from other American immigrants.

There are three types of immigrants: (1) long-term permanent residents, (2) new permanent immigrants, and (3) circular immigrants. In fact, studies show that, with the exception of Cubans, large numbers of Hispanic immigrants—whether documented or undocumented—are circular migrants. They are individuals traveling between two monolingual societies. Since the Hispanic population is a young population (42 percent are under the age of eighteen), many of these individuals are children traveling between two monolingual school systems. American school systems have never been, and probably will never be, operated using two languages as the media of instruction. The question which must be addressed by policy makers and educators is how best to prepare Hispanic children so that they can participate fully in an English-speaking social system when living in the United States and in a Spanish-speaking social system when living in the homeland. However, the fact is that, in the United States, schools must train for participation in an English-speaking social system, and in the homeland for a Spanish-speaking one.

The issue of creating and implementing bilingual education policy for Hispanics is further complicated by the fact that in a society that is committed to equality for all its participants, it is difficult to differentiate among different types of immigrants who may, in fact, have different needs. The permanent immigrant may need bilingual education only as a transition to English language skills.

While it can be argued that the individual benefits psychologically from knowing and appreciating his native language and culture, it may be just as strongly argued that society should not fund programs of cultural enrichment for linguistic minorities at the expense of the majority population.

The difficulty in creating bilingual education policy is directly related to several issues. First is the decision, early in the history of the nation, that America should have English as its one official language. The reasons for this decision are evident: the founding fathers were rightfully concerned with creating a nation of one people with a common culture and government. The European experience in creating nation states provided ample proof that language loyalty was a key factor in fostering national loyalties. Secondly, the public school system, for almost two centuries, did succeed in teaching English to successive waves of immigrants. While the public school never provided the ideal education which the mythology of history has credited to it, the ultimate proof of its relative success was the fact that the immigrant children for the most part did learn English and adopted it as their only language. Thus, the concept of bilingual education is contrary to the American experience of 200 years.

Given the success of the American experiment, many find it difficult to accept the fact that it may not apply as successfully to all Americans. The argument is easily made that the Hispanics, like other immigrants, should learn the American language and, thus, assimilate into the mainstream of American society. However, the Hispanics' experience is different. Many of them became part of the American nation when the lands on which they lived were acquired by treaty and annexation. In addition, many constitute a circular migration stream. Unlike other American migrants, Hispanics are traveling between two monolingual societies—English and Spanish become of equal value to the individual. In the case of Puerto Ricans, this migration is taking place within national boundaries.

THE IMPORTANCE OF EQUAL EDUCATIONAL OPPORTUNITY

In the United States, it has been generally acknowledged that no public institution has a greater impact on the individual's place in society than the school. This was the rationale for states and local communities to invest large sums to finance public school systems. Between the ages of six and eighteen most American children spend most of their time in schools. Their social contacts, their concepts of knowledge, and their social values are largely derived from the schools. Early educational success or failure will greatly determine the student's concept of self and of his position in society. The importance of assuring every American child an equal educational opportunity was the guiding principle in *Brown vs. Board of Education*. Concluding that segregated schools were inherently unequal, the Supreme Court ruled state laws segregating black and white students in the school system to be unconstitutional. The ruling was followed by a decade of civil rights activities that put an end to segregated schools. Leaders in the black community repeatedly underscored the inequality of educational opportunity in segregated school

systems and the importance of equal educational opportunity in
achieving social and economic equality. In recent years, the
Spanish-speaking community has also focused its civil rights efforts on the public schools. Its leaders have decried the lack of
equal access to education for their people in the public schools.

Lack of Educational Achievement Among Hispanics—The concept of what constitutes sufficient education is not a pedagogical
but a sociological concept which varies with time and place.
Earlier immigrants to America needed to understand and speak
English but often had little need for other educational skills to
participate in the labor market. In today's highly technological
service economy, a high school diploma is often a minimum
requisite for even entry-level jobs.

Hispanics lag well behind other groups in American society in
educational achievement. Of the graduating age cohort in 1976,
87 percent of non-Hispanic Americans graduated from high
school, while only 68 percent of all Mexican-Americans and 64
percent of all Puerto Ricans (on the mainland) did so. And concerning Hispanic achievement in postsecondary education, of the
graduating age cohort in 1976, 34 percent of non-Hispanic Americans graduated from college with a bachelor's degree while only
4 percent of Puerto Ricans (on the mainland) and 11 percent of
Mexican-Americans did so.

The importance of this lack of educational achievement is
shown by unemployment among Mexicans and Puerto Ricans.
While 5.9 percent of the majority population were unemployed
in 1976, 16.3 percent of the Puerto Ricans (on the mainland)
and 11.1 percent of the Mexicans were unemployed. The statistics
are more dramatic among teenagers: among urban youth, 15 percent of the majority population were unemployed while 55.2
percent of the Puerto Ricans (on the mainland) and 24.3 percent
of the Mexicans were unemployed.

The Hispanics' low educational achievement may be a major
factor in preventing economic and, eventually, social assimilation
into majority American society. Many have argued that this
low educational achievement is directly related to the inadequacy
of bilingual education policy and programs.

Bilingual Education Act of 1968—The first bilingual program
in an American public school for Spanish-speaking children was

organized in 1963 at the Coral Way Elementary School in Miami for the children of the relatively affluent Cubans who had migrated to South Florida following the assumption of power by Fidel Castro in 1959. The program was supported not by public funds but by a grant from the Ford Foundation. However, the success of the program gave impetus to demands for bilingual education —primarily among Spanish-speaking communities. And in 1968— after much debate—Congress passed the bilingual education act, providing supplemental funding for school districts interested in establishing programs to meet the "special educational needs of large numbers of children of limited English-speaking ability in the United States." The children served under the act also had to be from low-income families. Funding was provided for programs, planning, teacher training, and programs operation— including bilingual education, early childhood education, adult education, dropout programs, vocational programs, and courses dealing with history and culture.

The Bilingual Education Act of 1974—The Bilingual Education Act of 1974, which superseded the 1968 act, was more explicit in intent and design. Children no longer needed to be from low-income families, a criterion that had previously prevented the law from meeting the needs of large numbers of children. The 1974 act also provided a definition of a bilingual education program:

> . . . instruction given in, and study of, English and to the extent necessary to allow a child to progress effectively through the educational system, the native language of the children of limited English-speaking ability, and such instruction is given with appreciation for the cultural heritage of such children, and, with respect to elementary school instruction, such instruction shall, to the extent necessary, be in all courses or subjects of study which will allow a child to progress effectively through the educational system.

The Equal Opportunity Act of 1974—In yet another legislative action related to bilingual education, the Equal Education Opportunity Act of 1974 listed six actions that the Congress defines as denials of equal educational opportunity. Among them is the failure of an educational agency to take appropriate action to overcome language barriers that impede equal participation by its students in its instructional program.

This act provided for the initiation of civil action by individuals who have been denied equal educational opportunity. Thus, it provided for the first time a direct statutory right of action to non-English-speaking persons seeking to vindicate their rights to equal educational opportunity through the institution of effective bilingual programs in public schools.

While efforts at the federal level have been limited, the implementation of bilingual education programs at the state level has been even more limited. Most state statutes define bilingual education as a transitional process to make the student a fluent speaker of English; only two states, New Mexico and Texas, define bilingual education as the preservation of the native language and culture as well as the acquisition of English language skills.

The 1974 Supreme Court Decision—In 1974 the Supreme Court ruled that Chinese students who did not know English well enough to be instructed in the language were excluded from receiving an education by a school system which did not provide instruction in their native language. Justice Douglas delivered the opinion of the court:

> Under these state-imposed standards there is no equality of treatment merely by providing students with the same facilities, text books, teachers, and curriculum; for students who do not understand English are effectively foreclosed from any meaningful education.
>
> Basic English skills are at the very core of what these public schools teach. Imposition of a requirement that, before a child can effectively participate in the educational program, he must already have acquired those basic skills is to make a mockery of public education. We know that those who do not understand English are certain to find their classroom experiences wholly incomprehensible and in no way meaningful.

The Civil Rights Act of 1974 and the *Lau vs. Nichols* case have been used by proponents of bilingual education as an argument for mandated bilingual education programs. In fact, they offer no pedagogical guidelines. All they do is mandate compensatory education for non-English speakers.

The Aspira Court Decree—Also in 1974, Aspira of New York, Inc. obtained a court decree making selection of Spanish-surnamed and Spanish-speaking children for Language Assessment Battery (LAB) Test mandatory. Before the consent decree, bilingual programs were not being given to all the children, only to those identified by the office of the superintendent. The court made it mandatory to give bilingual programs and education to all students who need it by giving all Spanish-surnamed and Spanish-speaking children the LAB test to determine which children need bilingual programs. It is too early to judge the effect of mandatory bilingual education on the Puerto Rican school children of New York, but the Aspira decree has set a precedent which could be significant for other cities.

THE LIMITATIONS OF BILINGUAL EDUCATION PROGRAMS

The Department of Health, Education, and Welfare memorandum of May 25, 1970, stipulated that school districts with more than 5 percent national origin minority group children have a legal obligation to provide equal educational opportunity for language minority students. Although the memorandum requires school districts to provide some form of language program to meet the needs of language minority children, it does not specify what type of program this should be. When a district has not provided an educational program for language minority students, the department has strongly suggested that a curriculum be developed which does not penalize language minority students for their language and culture.

At the present time there are several types of educational approaches which attempt to deal with the difficulties of language minority students. The first, English as a Second Language (ESL), attempts to make non-English-speaking children proficient in English by providing supplementary instructional sessions in English for a specified time. Instruction in all other classes is in English. ESL differs from foreign language instruction in that it is designed to meet the immediate communication needs of the students by providing them with skills needed to communicate with teachers and peers in the classroom. The ESL approach seems to work best in communities where children receive enough exposure outside of school to function as "native speakers of English" in a relatively short time.

Another strategy is that of bilingual education, which offers instruction in both languages in varying degrees: (1) transitional bilingualism, in which the child is placed out of the program after gaining basic mastery of the English language; (2) monoliterate bilingualism, in which aural-oral skills in both languages are taught, but reading and writing are taught in English only, as in the case with some American Indian languages; (3) partial bilingualism, in which fluency and literacy are offered in both languages, but the native language is restricted to certain subject areas—such as music and gym; (4) a full bilingual program, in which both languages are used as media of instruction for all subjects. An important characteristic of the full bilingual program is that these programs utilize both languages and teach about both cultures on an equal basis.

The premises behind ESL programs and bilingual education programs are drastically different. Bilingual programs are designed to build on a child's existing native language skills to develop English language skills while maintaining and enhancing native language skills. Generally, classes requiring cognitive development are taught in the native language until the child has mastered the English language. Afterwards both languages are used as the media of instruction.

ESL programs are designed solely to teach English language skills so that the student can function in an English monolingual school system. There is no effort to maintain native language and culture.

Opponents of special treatment of language minority students argue that bilingual programs will not provide enough incentives for the students involved to learn English quickly. They also cite a lack of evidence that these programs will be successful. This is difficult to address because most of the attempts to evaluate bilingual education have been very poor.

Evaluation of Bilingual Programs—Most evaluations of bilingual programs fall into two categories: those which attempt to prove that bilingual programs accomplish their objectives and those which attempt to evaluate the effect of the program on acquisition of the second language. Generally, the bilingual programs which have been evaluated appear to be meeting many of their objectives without hindering the development of English-speaking skills.

In general, the early research in bilingualism in the United States found that bilingual students were handicapped in terms of intellectual functioning. These early findings have been consistently used as an argument against bilingual education. However, a study reviewing the research on Spanish-speaking bilinguals in the Southwest found that bilingual subjects who had received lower scores on verbal and nonverbal group tests did not differ significantly from those of English monolinguals on a nonverbal intelligence test when socioeconomic status was controlled.

Several programs have shown that Hispanic students in a bilingual curriculum can progress at a faster rate than Hispanic students in an English-only curriculum. In a Texas project, this was precisely the result obtained. The San Antonio Independent School District, between 1965 and 1966, concluded that the children receiving instruction in both English and Spanish made gains in English vocabulary and grammar superior to those made by children in the special English-only program. Yet here, too, the thrust of the curriculum was the student's eventual transference to English as a primary language rather than the maintenance of his first tongue.

A similar result was obtained in a program operating in the El Paso public school system between 1966 and 1967. In this project, children receiving instruction in Spanish showed that they could achieve skills in English at a level equal to those of children receiving instruction in English.

In an Illinois experiment, children enrolled in a bilingual education program were compared to students in an ESL program. The results disproved the theory that children learned more English in a monolingual program.

In 1970, the Edgewood Independent School District of San Antonio demonstrated the effectiveness of bilingual education with preschoolers. To determine effectiveness, the intelligence quotients (IQs) of children between the ages of three and five were measured at various stages of the bilingual program and compared to those of children in two other preschool programs which were similar in all aspects but were monolingual. Again, the findings supported the use of a bilingual curriculum. Significant gains in IQ were achieved by the children in the bilingual program while they were not noticed among children in the regular program. When they entered first grade, children in the bilingual program could communicate equally well in English and Spanish.

In their evaluation report on bilingual centers funded in 1972, the Chicago Board of Education found that students taught in Spanish performed just as well as students taught in English. At the end of the program, results derived from test data and various evaluation instruments indicated that Spanish-speaking students in a program with a bilingual instruction component did much better than their counterparts in programs with no bilingual education component. In general, the students in bilingual programs exhibited more positive concepts of their own worth and a higher level of aspiration.

In spite of the positive results of bilingual education programs provided by these few studies, it is impossible to draw conclusive proofs of the success of bilingual education at the present time. However, recent analysis of the research literature on second language acquisition and second language learning seems to indicate that bilingualism has a positive effect on cognitive functioning.

A Bilingual Education Policy for Hispanic Children

Although federally funded bilingual education programs have existed since 1968, there is confusion among educators and policy makers regarding the term bilingual education. This confusion is reflected in goals and objectives which are not well defined, resulting in confusion in program implementation. Indeed, a variety of educational models and teaching methodologies are all classified as bilingual education efforts. However, most of the programs are not bilingual education programs because they do not attempt to make the student literate in two languages. Many of them are limited to teaching English as a second language and completely neglect maintenance and enhancement of the native language skills.

DEFINING BILINGUAL EDUCATION

Noel Epstein is correct in saying that the most important task before policy makers and educators is clarification of the goals and direction of policies. His own recent critique of bilingual education programs, *Language, Ethnicity, and the Schools*, is a clear example of the confusion about bilingual education policies and programs in this country. Epstein recommends the termination of bilingual education programs based on an evaluation of existing programs which he frankly admits are inadequately conceived and implemented. While Epstein admits bilingual education may be desirable, he argues that it should not be mandated by the federal government. A similar argument could be made against any federal role in education. However, existing legislative and fiscal structures in the United States call for a federal role in most educational programs.

Transition or Maintenance Programs—The reality is that the United States is not a bilingual society; the majority of Americans have no need to be bilingual. While one can argue the cultural and educational advantages of learning a second language, for the majority of Americans such knowledge is not an absolute need.

For native speakers of a language other than English, learning English is necessary to function fully in American society. For most immigrants to America, this requires a transitional bilingual program. These individuals will learn English through their native language. They may or may not choose to preserve the native language, but it can be argued that society should not bear the cost of such cultural and linguistic maintenance. It is not essential to the individual for participation in society. Given the limited resources available for education, it is difficult to make the case for maintenance bilingual programs at public expense except for the case of circular migrants.

For individuals who are circular migrants, it becomes essential to be bilingual in order to function in two monolingual societies. A large number of Hispanic migrants participate in the circular migration stream and may require bilingual maintenance programs.

Social Responsibility to Circular Migrants—It can be argued that American society has no responsibility to provide a special education to the circular migrant. In fact, many would argue that American citizens should benefit most from the American education system. By this standard, Puerto Ricans, American citizens traveling within national boundaries and attending schools in the monolingual cities on the island and the mainland, would be those most clearly entitled to publicly funded bilingual maintenance programs.

However, it could also be argued that all residents of an American community are entitled to a public education. In this case, other Hispanics in the circular migration stream should also be entitled to maintenance bilingual programs. This would be true of documented and undocumented aliens who pay taxes as do other residents to maintain local school systems.

It could be argued that the best way to assimilate an individual into American society is bilingual education. Even those who are not advocates of bilingual education agree with Joshua Fishman that the schools seldom succeed in language maintenance: education in both the native and majority language results in the dominance of the majority language. The bilingual individual would choose the language of the majority society. There is little danger of bilingual education resulting in a monolingual Hispanic community alienated from majority society.

Equal educational opportunity does not necessarily mean the same educational experience; it means a diversity of educational experience to respond to the diversity of needs in a heterogeneous society. Only such a diversity of educational experience can enable the individual to have equal opportunity for social and economic advancement. The chief "Americanizing" force in the past has been the access to opportunity.

Summary

Before a proper educational policy can be created for the millions of Hispanics in America, two questions must be answered. The question of whether bilingual education is a proper and effective remedy for the problems of school failures among Hispanics cannot be answered without serious research and evaluation.

In order to evaluate the effectiveness of bilingual education for Hispanics, it must be determined whether Hispanic students master both the English and the Spanish language in bilingual programs; whether bilingual programs increase the students' achievement in other subjects; and what percentage of such students graduate from high school and continue on to college, in contrast to those Hispanic students not in a bilingual program.

These questions must be better answered by researchers who control for the degree of successful implementation. Researchers need to know whether adequate prior planning has taken place, whether or not participants understand the goals and methods of the program, and whether or not the program has adequate staff and materials. The quality and quantity of staff training programs need to be assessed, as does support for the program within the district and the community. Unrealistic goals and objectives based on inadequate knowledge of the methodology of bilingual education cause frustration among students and faculty which in turn sometimes leads to inadequate efforts to implement the program.

Only after bilingual programs have passed an "implementation test" should they be evaluated. In addition, the evaluations should take place over a period of years with properly developed instruments. Language development is a long process and should be treated accordingly.

Some would argue that one should not move into massive programs in bilingual education until proper evaluations of programs have been completed. However, it could be argued that there is enough preliminary evidence to support continuing implementation of bilingual education for Hispanic children while such programs are being evaluated. Lack of such diversity in education can be a criticism leveled at a number of federally mandated programs. Based on research and evaluation, federal policy and programs can better respond to individual community need. Financially beleaguered school systems hard pressed to implement programs for the majority population are going to find it difficult—if not impossible—to provide bilingual education for Hispanics without federal assistance. But federal assistance can be provided with the flexibility to respond to individual community needs.

Nathan Glazer

5

Politics of a Multiethnic Society

Twelve years ago, Daniel P. Moynihan and I, viewing the condition of politics in New York City, described two paradigms, which we dubbed for convenience as a "northern" and a "southern." We might more specifically have defined them as the northern urban pattern and some selected aspects of southern political reality as it emerged between the end of Reconstruction and the success of the civil rights acts and the voting rights acts in bringing blacks into the pattern of southern politics. We described the two patterns—and it should be recalled we were writing while we were in the midst of the explosion of racial violence in northern and western cities that marked the later 1960s and that only came to an end at the beginning of the 1970s—as follows:

> We now have as alternatives two models of group relations, which we will name the Northern and the Southern. Both reject a total assimilation in which group reality disappears. In the southern model, society is divided into two segments, black and white. The line between them is rigidly drawn. Other groups must choose to which segment they belong, even if . . . they do not really want to belong to either. Violence

NATHAN GLAZER *is professor of education and sociology at Harvard University and coeditor of* The Public Interest. *Dr. Glazer has taught at the University of California at Berkeley, Bennington College, Smith College, and at the Salzburg Seminar. He has received many scholarly honors and authored or edited over ten books, including* Beyond the Melting Pot *and* Affirmative Discrimination.

is the keynote of relations between the groups. And "separate but equal" is an ideology if not a reality.

The northern model is quite different. There are many groups. They differ in wealth, power, occupation, values, but in effect an open society prevails for individuals and for groups. Over time a substantial and rough equalization of wealth and power can be hoped for . . . and each group participates sufficiently in the goods and values and social life of a common society so that all can accept the common society as good and fair. There is competition between groups, as between individuals, but it is muted, and groups compete not through violence but through effectiveness in organization and achievement. Groups and individuals participate in a common society. Individual choice, not law or rigid custom, determines the degree to which any person participates, if at all, in the life of an ethnic group. . . . This is at any rate the ideal—prejudice and discrimination often force people into closer association with groups than they wish.

I will not suggest there is anything timeless about this contrast: as I have indicated, it was written, if one may be hyperbolic, in the blaze of northern urban ghettos, and at a time when the theme of "separate but equal" under which whites had kept down blacks had been startlingly resurrected by northern blacks under a different slogan, "black power," one which in its concrete details emphasized both separation from all whites, even potential allies, and an insistance on a turf in which blacks could wield independent power, whether or not that amounted to equal, more, or less power than whites wielded. I would not deny our political intention of showing the superiority of the northern pattern in which we had both grown up, or that we used a rhetorical device to meld the "separate but equal" of white supremacists and the "black power" of black separatists, both of which seemed to find resort to violence easy, into a single southern pattern.

And yet, despite the limitations of our now twelve-year-old formulation, I think there is much merit in it. I will replace the emphasis we placed then on *violence* in our description of the southern pattern by another feature that equally connects the pre-civil-rights-revolution South and the post-civil-rights-revolution United States: an emphasis on law as specifically defining the rights and privileges and burdens of two groups, which are assumed to encompass all of society; one is a favored group, the other a disfavored one, and law addresses each group as a group and asserts what one owes to the other. Pre-civil-rights southern law protected the privileges of the white group; post-civil-rights national law tries to advance the position of the black group. With this modification, I will argue that one can see the present situation in group relations as one that is still understandable in terms of a conflict between the two patterns with the rise, in the sidelines, of what we may murkily discern as a third, complicating pattern.

We have thus seen an evolution of the southern pattern, in the 1970s, into a rather more benign form, but still one marked off from the northern urban pattern. But we are now moving into a situation in which a third pattern is emerging—shall we call it the western?—and we may expect now a tripolar struggle among different ways of conceiving and adapting to American ethnic diversity.

One possible pattern, a model to which liberals and nationalists once aspired, that of assimilation, pure and simple, in which people act in politics on the basis of any interest but ethnic or racial group interest simply does not seem to be in the cards for the immediate future. Each of the three patterns that has replaced it operates instead on the reality that we are not a homogeneous society, ethnically or racially or religiously, and that the conflicts of class and interest that dominate all democratic politics are in the American situation affected by a clash of ethnic and racial and religious interests which are not simply reflections of economic interest. They are interests that are based in part on the dominant socioeconomic characteristics of each group but which also reflect in varying degrees values of each group which themselves become interests. In what way, for example, can we interpret the now severe conflicts over abortion and school prayer, or over school busing, as conflicts based on *economic* interest? Indeed, on occasion one sees people acting directly against their economic interests to realize their value objectives. If—as I believe is true—the opponents of abortion are predominantly white upper-working and lower-middle class, and the supporters are the more educated and more liberal parts of the population, and if opposition to government-funded abortion means more infants added to the welfare population and higher taxes for the working and middle classes, opponents of government-funded abortion act against their economic interests. But this has hardly moderated the intensity of opposition to abortion. Similarly, the intensity of passions over such value issues as prayer and gun control can hardly be given an economic meaning, and there is only limited economic significance to the fierce opposition to busing that rends many communities.

But, returning to our two patterns, the southern pattern is one that takes for granted the primacy of *one* central division in society, between white and black. The white South was ethnically much more homogeneous than the rest of the country, with only moderate infusions of southern and eastern European immigrants and very few Chinese and Japanese immigrants to complicate the stark black-white division. Where there were European ethnic groups (e.g., Italians in New Orleans, Jews in many cities) they simply became part of the white majority, willy-nilly. They shared in the advantages given by legal segregation and formal discrimination (we will not get into the argument of whether Italians and Jews were worse off or better off because of it), and similarly American Indians and Chinese were assimilated by white prejudice and insistence into the lower black caste.

Inevitably such a stark division in society meant that every issue had to be seen in black and white terms (in both senses), and since one group was held down in an inferior position, violence, whether exercised legally as in the practices of the police force or illegally through lynching and threat, was part of the political reality. When we argued in the second edition of *Beyond the Melting Pot* in 1970 that the southern pattern was moving north, we had in mind the spread of interracial violence as exemplified in the riots. But this was not an essential part of the southern pattern. What was essential was the sharp division between two groups, and only two groups, and the significance of law in defining the rights and privileges of each group. Law in the South codified intergroup relations; we now have a national system of law affecting the relations of groups in various spheres. But looking back at the distinction we made in 1969, I would argue that one evidence of the migration of the southern pattern into the North and West is that intergroup relations, once regulated by custom, custom which hardly dared to pronounce publicly the specific roles and expectations which guided intergroup relations, are now defined in law. The law in question is very different from the law that governed black-white relations and kept blacks in an inferior position in the South; it is a law designed to achieve equality and not to ensure dominance. But it shares one thing in common with that earlier law: it names groups, and because they are named, individuals inevitably become beneficiaries or nonbeneficiaries of the law specifically because of group membership. As that previous southern law did, it defines who has the right to claim the benefits of membership in a group and who must accept the lack of benefit because he is defined as part of another group. The southern pattern, to my mind, is exemplified by the fact that there are two groups—one group to benefit, another to be deprived of benefits.

The complication created in the North and West (and with increasing immigration and economic growth, in the South, too) is that instead of simply two groups, in reality there are many groups. Thus, there are groups that must be added to the benefited groups (Asians, Hispanics) whose "right" to be so included is challengeable; and groups incorporated into the nonbenefited category who attack and criticize their placement (Italians, Poles, Jews) and indeed some of whom are able to get themselves shifted from the nonbenefited to the benefited group (Asian Indians, for example).

I have suggested the term "western" (or "southwestern") pattern for this developing situation of *two* groups of groups, the benefited and the nonbenefited, because it is in those states that the complications of applying the southern pattern come sharply into view. Thus, it will be recalled that quite early in desegregation cases the question arose, are the Hispanics to be considered majority or minority. If the first, then it was possible to have "desegregated" schools in which black and Hispanic together comprised the entire student body. If the latter, there were new complications. When the groups to be desegregated rose to three, two of which were themselves a combination of other groups (the Hispanic and the Asian, as in San Francisco), the problem became even more complicated.

Let us now summarize our three patterns in terms of how they envisage the group structure of society. The northern pattern, I would argue, sees American society as a mixture of many groups, that can be ranged along many spectra, of which perhaps the most significant are those of income and occupation. But there are other spectra, too, for example, political influence. It was characteristic of the developing urban political patterns in the

North that groups that were far from the top in occupation, status, and income did become dominant politically—for example, the Irish in Boston and in other cities. Associated with this multigroup spectrum was a system of law that did not recognize differences among groups, a system of law that aimed at formal blindness to ethnic, racial, and religious difference. This is not to say that the law was not used to advance the interests of one group or another. In Boston, when the Irish became politically dominant, the still Yankee Protestant dominated state legislature created the Finance Commission to watch closely the operations of Boston city government and deprived Boston of a considerable measure of self-government. One could say that Yankee Protestants were, through law, reducing the power and independence of Irish Catholics—but the law itself adhered to universal forms and did not specify Irish Catholics as the deprived, Yankee Protestants as the benefited. In one case, law did differentiate among the various groups by name, in the case of immigration law, but that was considered, from the 1920s on, an egregious case of group discrimination, finally removed in 1965. The northern pattern, then, assumes a spectrum of groups and law that is blind in distinguishing among them.

The southern pattern, in contrast, envisages two groups, and the law has never been blind between them. For centuries it specified an inferior position, and then, almost immediately, with no period of color blindness intervening, it defined a position of special protection. At this point, I make no argument that this was an error; indeed, one may argue that it was an inevitability. If blacks were separated from whites in schools, there might indeed have been no other way of overcoming the heritage of that past than to specify the proportions of white and black that would be allowable in each school. Or if blacks were deprived of political representation, there might have been no alternative to defining what was a satisfactory level of political representation except by specifying that if there were x percent black in a community, there could not be less than x percent representatives in the city council. Whether in these two cases this was the right course or the best course or the constitutionally required course are questions I will for the moment put aside. It was the course that came into existence and that in varying degrees spread through the country.

I have argued that we now see emerging a western or south-western pattern, one which is distinguished from the northern pattern with its spectrum of groups. If there are more than one, two, or three disfavored groups, complications arise that mean the southern pattern cannot apply. There are a number of reasons. One reason is that the disfavored are disfavored in varying degrees, on the basis of different histories and different legal statuses. The American Indian has a unique status in that this is the only group with sharp definition and policing of its boundaries in law. Indians may be these days the beneficiaries of substantial sums in compensation for land-taking. They may possess through their status as members of tribes important nat-ural resources. Who is an Indian, who is not, and of what tribe become important in defining these beneficiaries. They are also beneficiaries of affirmative action policies, but these pale in sig-nificance when compared with the substantial sums to which individuals may have a legal claim as a consequence of tribal membership.

Hispanics are a congeries of groups, each with different legal, social, economic, and political characteristics. The Puerto Ricans are in an ambiguous condition of citizenship—full citizens on the mainland, but of a special status if they live in Puerto Rico—and a simple passage in either direction shifts them from one to the other, and as often as they move from island to mainland, so often is their political status changed. Mexican-Americans have various statuses—from old settlers (some with special treaty protection) to recent immigrant citizens to immigrants legally domiciled to illegal immigrants. They stand as a group higher than the Puerto Ricans economically and exercise more political influence. Cubans are another special category, perhaps closest to earlier European immigrants. They begin as political refugees, and their middle-class social status (and perhaps the additional benefits they receive from government as favored political ref-ugees) has rapidly moved them above both Puerto Ricans and Mexican-Americans in occupation, income, and, where they are sufficiently concentrated, political influence. It is unnecessary to move through other groups of Hispanics who are becoming numerically important in one or another part of the country—Dominicans, Nicaraguans, Salvadoreans, Columbians, and others, for each of whom a slightly different story must be told.

And finally, consider the multiplicity of Asian groups and their varying socioeconomic positions and histories. When Asians were first included in affirmative action programs, it was because there had been a history of severe legal discrimination against Chinese and Japanese and because they, too, were of a nonwhite race. Presumably, consistency required that all nonwhite races that had suffered official discrimination be included among the protected groups. I am less clear about why they were included as protected groups in the revision of the Voting Rights Act of 1975, since there was, I believe, no evidence that where their numbers permitted (e.g., Hawaii) they suffered from political discrimination or underrepresentation.

Whatever the justification for including Asians as beneficiaries of legislation and regulation that was devised in response to the southern pattern primarily to raise the position of blacks, it must become much muddier when we add to Chinese and Japanese— who were almost all the Asians we had at the time of the major civil rights legislation of the mid-1960s—substantial and rapidly growing communities of Filipinos, Koreans, Asian Indians, Vietnamese, and some smaller Asian groups. It would take us too far afield to describe the varying legal statuses and socioeconomic positions of each of these groups, and I am not clear to what degree they fall under the protections offered in various laws and regulation to Asian-Americans, aside from the general protection offered to all by our major antidiscriminatory legislation.

In any case, the first distinguishing characteristic of the new western or southwestern pattern is that we have swept up under the rubric of the protected group a range of groups, some of whose rights to special benefit and protection are disputed by others, both among the protected and the nonprotected. This differentiates it from the southern pattern.

And differentiating the western from the northern pattern is the fact that these new ethnic strains added to our national mix do not form a part of a single multiethnic spectrum; both because of law and because of other factors which we will have to explore, there is a break between the white majority (whatever the number of ethnic groups into which it can be divided) and the new immigrant groups of different race and cultural background.

This break reflects the fact that the dominant European ethnic groups completed their immigration to this country almost sixty years ago. European immigration then came to a halt for more than two decades. When it resumed, in the post–World War II years, it was moderate in size, and the new immigrants—Irish, Germans, Italians, Jews, Poles, Ukrainians—in large measure either affiliated themselves with the ethnic groups already established decades before or rapidly assimilated. One could be aware in the old immigrant areas of first settlement in the northeastern cities in the 1950s and 1960s that there were indeed new immigrants from the countries of Europe that had fed the immigration of the pre-1920s, but they did not become nationally visible, and there was no reason to think that whatever patterns of economic and political mobility and cultural and religious change that had affected earlier immigrants from their countries and made them into Americans of a familiar type would not operate on them.

The situation since the mid-1960s that has strengthened a nascent western or southwestern pattern is of a different type. The figures themselves tell the story. In the 1960s, there were 1.6 million European and Canadian immigrants, and in the 1970s, only 957,000, while Asian immigration jumped from 362,000 in the 1960s to 1.5 million in the 1970s. Immigration from Mexico rose from 432,000 to 624,000, from South America, only from 219,000 to 266,000—but we are all aware that substantial numbers of illegal immigrants have come from Latin America. Even immigration from Africa, only 33,000 in the 1960s, rose to 87,000 in the 1970s.

The point of this recital of facts, discussed in more detail in chapter 2 by Charles Keely, is that this growing diversity of immigration and the shift from European and Canadian sources to Latin American, Asian, and African must create a new and different multiethnic pattern. The new pattern mirrors neither the northern, based on European strains, all of whom have become assimilated, whatever the emotional and nostalgic ties to home countries, nor the southern, with its stark black-white gulf based on the history of slavery and casteism.

What consequences will all this have on the American political pattern? Large consequences will be left for the conclusion. But at the moment, one can see unrolling fascinating clashes, with equally indignant responses by those raised in the northern pattern and those who are utilizing the new conceptions that arose out of the southern pattern to overturn northern assumptions and practices.

Nothing is as revealing as the conflict over the redistricting of council seats in New York City which led a federal court to suspend New York's 1981 primary elections and the Supreme Court to confirm its judgment on the very eve of the election. There have been suspensions of elections in southern cities over similar issues—how to redistrict to guarantee a certain number of seats for blacks, conflicts over at-large and district seats, or conflicts over annexations that could dilute black votes. They received little national attention. It was understood that in the context of the southern pattern, where white stood arrayed against black and national power was inserted to help blacks, such conflicts would occur, with interventions to increase black power and reduce white power. (I leave aside the question whether this assumption was always justified.)

The North is a rather more complex matter, as we have argued, and its complexity, when the Voting Rights Act of 1965 was used to cover some counties of New York City, was already revealed when Hasidic Jews charged that a redistricting intended to increase the number of black congressional seats from Brooklyn had, by splitting their community into two districts, reduced *their* political power. A third party had entered the suit (any close study of the situation would undoubtedly have revealed many more political groups with the potential to enter). In any event, the Supreme Court upheld the redistricting; a new district designed to produce a new black congressman came into being— and it has regularly voted into office a Jewish manufacturer, even though it has had on occasion excellent black candidates offered with which to replace him. The stark black-white conflict had been complicated not only by the Hasidic community, but by the fact that white candidates could appeal, against the assumptions of the southern pattern, to black voters—just as we have seen, in the North and West, the reverse, with black candidates winning in majority white districts.

The more recent New York City situation was even more complex. Here we not only have in play a variety of racial and ethnic groups (blacks and Puerto Ricans in particular), but strictly political considerations, such as the desire of incumbent councilmen in New York City to preserve their seats under redistricting. The New York City councilmanic redistricting was a classic case of black, white, and Puerto Rican incumbents against challengers, black, white, and Puerto Rican, using the time-tested forms of gerrymandering, a technique that goes back to Massachusetts long before there were immigrant communities, blacks, or Puerto Ricans to complicate the issue. The mayor of New York knew that in the new situation he had to protect his flank against minority attacks—and did, or so he thought. Leading blacks, including Congressman Charles E. Rangel; Kenneth B. Clark, distinguished community leader; and Herman D. Farrell, the black Manhattan Democratic leader (the successor to the great Tammany chieftains), all supported the redistricting, as did Puerto Rican Councilman Gilberto Gerena-Valentin. Gerena-Valentin changed his mind and sued (as did others) on grounds of violation of the voting rights act. Interestingly enough, Gerena-Valentin was represented by Gabe Kaimowitz of the Puerto Rican Legal Defense and Education Fund—a lawyer who had achieved a certain measure of fame by bringing the "black English" case in the Ann Arbor School District of Michigan.

What is clear in the New York City case is that there was no "gang-up" of whites against blacks—the characteristic situation the voting rights act was designed to prevent. What happened was a new chapter in the lengthy and complex interplay among ethnicity, political interest, and public interest in New York City. It was claimed that the percentage of seats that would go to blacks and Puerto Ricans, in view of their substantial increase as a proportion of the population of New York City in ten years, would be too small under redistricting, and that the percentage of seats that would go to whites would be too large, in view of the fact that *their* proportion in the city population had dropped greatly since 1970.

The law permitted these challenges, the suspension of elections at a cost of millions of dollars, and the introduction of a great deal of confusion which—as against the very intention of the law —*reduced* substantially the numbers voting in the primary when it eventually took place. The situation to which it was applied had nothing to do with the intention of the law and was covered by what can only be considered accident. The law set a simple statistical standard for federal intervention, 50 percent of eligibles voting in a presidential election. But because (for reasons which are important but also somewhat obscure) very low proportions of blacks and Puerto Ricans register and vote in New York City, it is very difficult for the high minority boroughs to show 50 percent of eligibles voting. Thus they fall under the act.

But there is a serious problem when the act is employed. There is no way of guaranteeing that *any* percentage of blacks or Puerto Ricans will produce a black or Puerto Rican candidate, as the Brooklyn case shows. Councilman Theodore Silverman was chairman of the committee that approved the new districting; he himself represents a district that is majority black and Puerto Rican. Three adjacent districts, represented by two blacks and one Puerto Rican, had lost population. His had gained (a characteristic pattern for the 1970s, for while the black and Puerto Rican population has *increased,* the population of black and Puerto Rican districts had *declined* as blacks and Puerto Ricans spread to new sections of the city). Silverman asked, "So what would you add to those other districts? Some blacks from Mr. Silverman's district? Or some whites?" He had given up some blacks, he said, and the result had been to leave him with a district that was 60 percent black and Hispanic. The *New York Times* wrote, "The rule-of-thumb minimum for a black or Puerto Rican district is 70 percent, according to the council's mapmakers."

This rule of thumb is dependent on two factors. There is a huge age difference between white and black and Hispanic populations in New York City and in other central cities; children under eighteen cannot vote, and young people generally in their twenties and thirties do not vote as much as older people. But second, there are great differences in proportions of each group enrolled, and fewer voting-age blacks vote in New York than in Mississippi. This is an old story, known to every politician, long preceding the voting rights act and quite impervious to its intentions or assistance. Arthur Klebanoff pointed out in an unpublished paper that between 1950 and 1965, blacks and Puerto Ricans increased from 9 to 29 percent of the Brooklyn population, but this had almost no impact on representation.

The remnants of the older political machinery, once broad-based, continued to control Brooklyn politics as late as 1966. Jews and Italians ran the stores, owned the apartments, and filled the political clubhouses.

This was to be expected. The surprise was the absence of any competing Negro or Puerto Rican organizations. Jews and Italians continued in office long after the districts they represented became predominantly Negro and Puerto Rican.

What is even more surprising is that further massive increases in the percentage of black and Puerto Rican population in the fifteen years since 1966 have not been accompanied by any substantial increase in minority representation. It is the roots of this phenomenon that must be explored, and they cannot be overcome by the brute intervention of a hardly relevant voting rights act. The realities that have created this situation are the demographic characteristics of minority and white populations, the failure for whatever reasons of blacks and Puerto Ricans to equal the economic and skill resources of the old immigrant populations, and perhaps some problems in organization in these communities that have cultural and historical roots. The Irish got into politics and with great effect. Jews did not, and it is only in recent decades they have been playing a substantial political role in the city in which they are by far the largest ethnic group. (Abraham Beame, elected in 1973, was, astonishingly, the first Jewish mayor of New York!) There are reasons for these substantial differences. They have no relation to the assumptions of the voting rights act.

And the situation Klebanoff described in 1966 persists. The *Wall Street Journal* asserted in an editorial: "Last year, 59.5 percent of all voting-age blacks in Mississippi voted, as did 51.3 percent of all voting-age blacks in South Carolina. The comparable figures were 40.4 percent for New York, and 38.4 percent for Massachusetts."

Thus, even under the best intentions to increase black and Puerto Rican representation, and it is agreed these intentions were hardly dominant, one would be hard put to see what kind of voting system in New York City could represent blacks and Puerto Ricans in any proportion within hailing distance of their percentage of the city population. If one concentrated minorities up to 70 percent, it could be argued they were being concentrated in classic fashion to reduce their influence. And even if one did so, and if Puerto Ricans and blacks were divided in the district, what was to prevent a politically astute white with money or political attractiveness or both from gaining the seat?

The *New York Times* in an editorial pointed to the complexities of determining what was fair, or indeed what was
effective, in redistricting. Silverman had given up some blacks in
his new district. Said the *Times*:

> Was the change intended to promote a white man's chances for re-election?
> Without the change, the district would have become even more black.
> Or was moving the black voters to the adjacent district intended to
> promote a black woman's chance for re-election? Many whites have moved
> into her district since 1970, reducing the black plurality that had elected
> Mary Pinkett.
>
> Should fairness be measured by how many districts are likely to elect
> minority candidates, or by how many contain more nonwhites than
> whites? The two can be quite different. Poorer black and Hispanic voters
> concentrated in some areas are less likely to vote than middle-class voters
> in others. And minority voters who do turn out may prefer a white
> candidate. Despite efforts to create a black state assembly seat in central
> Harlem, Edward Sullivan, a white, keeps on winning.

The newspapers explored well the complexities involved in
applying the southern pattern to the northern mosaic, but even
so they left aside other complexities. There were splits within
each of the groups. For example, there were splits between the
two minority groups, and there were differing interests among
the whites. It is hardly likely that in the complexities of New
York City politics the issue in the city council was seen as one
of only "whites" against "minorities." It could not have been a
matter of indifference whether that white was Jewish, Italian, or
Irish. But since all whites had been reduced by the southern
simplicities of the voting rights act to the position of homogeneous
defendants, no one explored these complexities—they were not at
issue legally, significant as they may have been in affecting some
of the redistricting.

Is the distinction between the southern pattern and the northern
pattern more than academic? Is it of significance for the actual
condition of blacks and Hispanics that a southern mode overtakes
a northern mode? I believe it is. The southern mode forces everything into the courts and into a context of rights and wrongs.
In the courts one side is right, and the other is wrong; there are
no alternatives. Outside the courts, there is bargaining and negotiation. How does one bargain when one is a minority, one might
ask. The fact is in the northern pattern one is a minority among
other minorities. And no minority, in a situation where formal

equality prevails, where all have access to the ballot, where all have access to the schools and colleges, and in particular the law schools, is fully powerless. There are areas in which a group, even a small group and a poor one, is dominant, and has influence—as the Hasidic Jews in the Williamsburg section of Brooklyn do. To push the question of the practical significance of the two patterns further, is it more helpful to get a decision from a court that one is right, or an outcome to a negotiation in which one gets something—a new housing project or school, a nomination for an assembly seat, a promise of a job as an assistant district attorney? I have described the common coin of the northern pattern. Negotiation is not ruled out by the use of the southern pattern—one can still negotiate before, during, and after a court decides one is right or wrong. But it does encourage a different kind of combat, a different kind of stance. An adversary lawyer working for a foundation- or public-funded legal defense organization is a very different kind of battering ram with which to expand the opportunities of a group than a community leader. For one thing, he very likely is of a different ethnic group, does not live in the community, has a rather abstract idea of how it may be advanced. His participation does not make it easy to negotiate and compromise.

Clearly, in the South of the 1940s, 1950s, and 1960s, and perhaps even in the 1970s, that is just what one wanted; since negotiation and compromise in a situation of political powerlessness would get nowhere, it was essential to appeal to the Constitution and the law, to fight the crucial issues through the courts, and one wanted the best lawyer, rather than a representative of the people (not that there is necessarily a division between the two—it depends on the circumstances).

I believe the political process that in the end made way for the Jews, the Italians, the Poles, and the other immigrant groups of the second immigration would in time—did in time—make way for the blacks and the Puerto Ricans. The process will not come to an end because we now have national laws based on the experience of the South to which new groups can appeal. But it is also true that when another and apparently more effective way is opened up, an older way tends to fall into a certain degree of disuse. And that will have consequences, too.

The political problem of the northern black today is not a

problem of formal inequality through rule or actual inequality through custom. The polls are open, the courts are open, the civil service is open—indeed, under the new affirmative action measures of recent years, more than open—the colleges and law schools are open. Despite all this, there is a severe problem, one best symbolized by the remarkably low registration and voting figures of blacks in the northern cities, much lower as we have seen than the percentages in the South. The matter is mystifying. It cannot be explained by arguing blacks are such a small minority in the northern cities that politics is for them a futile path to the advancement of group interests. Indeed, blacks in northern cities form as high or higher a percentage of the population as they do in Mississippi and South Carolina, where they are far more active at the polls. Nor is the problem poverty; blacks of the southern states are no more prosperous. Nor is it poor education; the black of the North is better educated. Nor is it that there are no models to encourage political participation; there have been major models in the form of prominent black congressmen, assemblymen, councilmen, and state officials for a good forty years or more.

I hesitate to suggest reasons for this remarkable phenomenon. Perhaps one reason is the rise of federally-funded poverty organizations in the 1960s which were for the most part limited to blacks and minorities and which gave jobs and access to federal funds. These may have been seen as a more desirable way of advancement, and, as a result, traditional politics was neglected. As these programs decline in access to funds and are wound down, we may see a new rise in involvement in traditional politics. Perhaps, too, another factor which discouraged involvement in local politics was the fact that the national government for twenty years was the standard bearer of minority rights. The federal largess was such that it seemed more valuable to enter the federal civil service in the newer programs than to start out on the hard career of local political representation. A leadership cadre that had been available to earlier ethnic groups in the days when the federal government did almost nothing for the cities may have been drawn off into federal office holding. Once again, the refusal of the Reagan administration to continue in the line of the Kennedy, Johnson, Nixon, Ford, and Carter administrations may force a new rebirth of black and Hispanic participation in local politics. I include the Nixon-Ford administrations in this sequence because, from the point of view of federal programs aiding minorities, there was no break in growth, whether in money distributed or positions funded, during those years. Indeed, those were the years when affirmative action and the agencies enforcing it (Office of Federal Contract Compliance, Equal Employment Opportunity Commission) grew rapidly.

I have suggested that a third pattern is visible on the horizon, which I have dubbed the western or southwestern. What are the characteristics of this pattern?

First, the newer groups are more distant in culture, language, and religion from white Americans, whether of the old or new immigrations, than these were from each other. We now have what are in American terms groups more exotic than ever before. Added to Chinese and Japanese are now Filipinos, Koreans, Asian Indians, Vietnamese, Cambodians, Laotians, and Pacific Islanders, speaking languages unconnected to the languages of Europe (though some of the Asian-Indian languages are of course Indo-European), practicing religions that have had very few representatives in this country (though there are many Christians among them), and of racial or ethnic stocks distant from the European. The largest of these new groups is of course the Mexican, which does not qualify as exotic in these ways, but when one takes into account the substantial Indian component in the Mexican immigration, this does add an element of distance. Mexican culture itself, because of the Indian-Spanish mix, strikes Europeans and Americans as something quite new and different.

Second, issues of legality of immigration loom large for this new immigrant pattern. This was never an issue for the old immigration, or indeed for most of the new. Immigration to this country was in effect almost unregulated until the early 1920s, getting citizenship was easy, and thus almost everyone was legal. Certainly the question of legality which affects many of the new groups of the West and Southwest raises many issues and affects deeply their ability to participate in politics.

Third, the new groups enter a situation in which the differences between groups--in income, occupation, educational achievement, language, and voting participation—have become national political issues. They have a right to bilingual education —whether they want it or not (and if they have a right to it, many in the group will find it to their advantage to claim the right, at least for the others). They have a right (most of them) to assistance in voting in their own language. They are protected by antidiscrimination legislation, as are all Americans, but further have varying claims to special consideration under affirmative action requirements.

Fourth, I sense a remarkable diversity among them in their capacity to take advantage of American economic and educational opportunities for upward mobility. Despite the differences among the old immigrants (Irish and German), they tended to settle in different areas, and the differences did not lead to marked political conflict between them. Despite the differences among the new immigrants (Jews and Italians were the most prominent groups among them), they too did not become antagonists. I sense we may see something new among the new immigrants. Some show a surprising mobility. Some of course come fairly highly educated and in professional statuses (Asian Indians, for example); some show remarkable ability in small business (Koreans); some already show considerable success in educational advancement. But the gaps that these differential achievements open up between these groups and the two great minorities, black and Hispanic (or, specifically, the Mexican and Puerto Rican element among the Hispanics), suggest conflict among new immigrant groups, as well as between them and older Americans. The matter becomes more delicate insofar as these differences are seen crudely as a result of differential discrimination. Such a perception is an effect of antidiscrimination and affirmative action legislation and regulations and the way they are interpreted by courts and regulators. A competition over who is more discriminated against, who more worthy of federal or other protection, may well develop, with nasty overtones.

Finally, there is an important international dimension to the new immigration that must be considered. A few years ago, after hearing testimony on immigration to the United States, a congressman summed up the matter by saying, "We have been told that by the end of the century there will be 140 million Mexicans, and half of them will be living north of the Rio Grande." Perhaps those figures are too high—perhaps there will only be 100 million and only a third of them will be living north of the Rio Grande. I leave it to demographers to figure out which is the more likely prospect. But we will have on our southern border a neighbor, still poorer than we are by a considerable margin, with grounds enough, old and new, for resentment of the United States; with an enormous minority across the border; and with the right to be educated in American schools in language and loyalty to Mexico, in its history, its culture, and its customs (I speak only of the *right,* now fairly well established—many things may come to pass before it is fully exploited in all respects, including some narrowing of the right). One recalls that a few hundred thousand Japanese, with their homeland 7,000 miles away, helped give rise to a great fear of the "Yellow Peril." (The actual growth of Japanese power was a more substantial factor.) I am farthest from issuing any call to alarm or suggesting that troubles, if they arise, will be Mexico's fault rather than ours. But it is only necessary to say the situation is potentially delicate and neither the old nor the new immigrations from Europe or from Canada raised any parallel issue.

On this international dimension, two substantial new communities in the United States—Cubans and Vietnamese—have been created not as a result of our will, but as a result of decisions of foreign powers over which we had no control. In both cases, we responded in accord with old traditions, newly strengthened, of offering asylum to refugees and a place to live to immigrants. But recall that that tradition suffered a substantial interruption of at least fifty years in the middle of this century, and some groups—Chinese and Japanese—were barred from immigration for very much longer periods. There are many countries in the world in which the expulsion of large parts of their population—ethnic or racial minorities, political dissidents—may seem desirable in years to come. How will we respond when it is not a few hundred thousand Cubans or Vietnamese, but a few million _____ (fill in as the spirit moves you)? This possibility of expulsion of immigrants to the United States is not an unlikely one, and we must consider how it will complicate intergroup relations in the United States.

These five factors to my mind create a heady brew, and, turbulent as was the assimilation of the new European immigrant groups, the tensions of these five factors suggest a more turbulent period for the new groups. They will, on the one hand, form more obvious targets for attack; they will, on the other, find easier access to legal protection and legal rights that are unique in the experience of older Americans and which will create resentment. The combination, to my mind, spells a good deal of trouble which we have not yet seen but which, in the absence of good sense and adaptability, may yet come.

The first pattern of race relations described, the northern, found a resolution, at least as far as the European immigrants went. Whatever the intensity of conflict between immigrant groups, in time a modus vivendi was worked out. While each group maintained its attachments to its culture and its homeland, to some degree (in the case of Israel, it amounts to an overriding political commitment) it was able to find a place in American economy, society, and polity. If the groups analyzed the statistics, they might have found much to grouse about. Since the Irish dominated electoral politics, all other groups were that token "deprived." Since the Jews were the most successful in terms of high occupational status, all the others were by that token "deprived." Yet that is not the way the political debate went, and all the European ethnic groups believed they had done well in America; there is scarcely a one that bears grievances.

The northern pattern might well have accommodated the blacks as they moved North, the Puerto Ricans as they emigrated to the mainland, the Mexican-Americans as they moved into the cities of the West. It has not been successful in doing so in the perception of minority leaders and of leaders of opinion for the majority. Actually, as economist Thomas Sowell has recently documented, the success of the northern pattern of accommodation and mobility independent of direct public assistance was greater than is generally realized. I will not rehearse the facts of black and other minority group political, economic, and educational status, but every average, we must realize, conceals within it substantial groups well above the average. The fact that young black families do almost as well in income these days as young white families seems a substantial achievement (and it was already becoming apparent when Moynihan and I were writing the introduction to the second edition of *Beyond the Melting Pot* twelve years ago).

In saying that what we have had is in part a failure in perception, I do not dispute that there is a failure in reality in bringing blacks into the mainstream of American society and opportunity. But the failure is not only one in reality. The partial successes of reality are now swept away by prevailing perceptions. These perceptions shape the actions of major government agencies, the interpretations of the major television networks, and the major organs of the press. They are now as much reality as any reality. And as a result, the southern pattern has become, in its new formulation in which law is designed to raise the lower caste rather than keep it down, the national pattern.

I have argued that this new national pattern will be challenged as a new wave of immigration reshapes American cities. The new wave will raise many questions. Does it deserve the same benefits as the protected classes of the 1960s? How will the borders of protected classes be set? If nonwhite immigrants have greater benefits in law than white natives, what will that do to the willingness to allow immigration to continue at the rate of the 1970s? As some of these immigrants show success in economic activity and in achieving political representation, what will that do to the viability of the southern pattern?

Beyond all three patterns is one we have not even mentioned, the ideal of the period of Americanization of World War I, the 1920s, and the 1930s. The ideal was one of full assimilation of all immigrant groups to a common cultural type, so that ethnicity would play no role in individual consciousness, groups would not be formed around ethnic interests, "hyphenated Americanism" would be a thing of the past, and the United States would be as homogeneous in its Americanness as the nations of the old world were in their Englishness, their Frenchness, their Germanness, their Italianness.

Leave aside the fact that the old Americans did not seem to hold this ideal in full consistency. They expected abandonment of difference, but would not make a payoff of full acceptance of those who had given up their difference. Leave aside the fact that even the nations of the old world have lost their homogeneity, to the extent they had it, under the impact of the economic changes of the past three decades. Leave aside the realism of expecting people to give up ethnic attributes, attachments, and loyalties within any brief period of time. This still is an ideal that is worth holding in mind and presenting as probably the best outcome for America. Difference, alas, almost always becomes a source of conflict. Assimilation has already proceeded so far with some groups, specifically the European ethnic groups, that it is not an unreasonable hope. If this original hope offered the best chance of a society in which ethnic and racial rivalries and conflicts could be laid to rest, there is no reason why it cannot still be held up as an ideal. Instead, it has been driven from the field of discussion of ethnic issues. The "melting pot" is now attacked not only on the empirical ground that it really did not melt that much or that fast, but on the normative ground that it should not have been allowed to do so. And on the basis of this attack, Americanization becomes a dirty word, and bilingualism and biculturalism receive government support.

I doubt that this is wise. Without endorsing the rigors of the Americanization programs of World War I and the succeeding decades, one can still see the virtue of forging a single society out of many stocks and can still see that this process deserves some public guidance. Beyond northern, southern, and western patterns, there is still, or should be, an ultimate goal which should guide us. Insofar as we have one, it seems to be first, that every group must match every other group in economic resources, occupational status, political representation, and distribution through cities and metropolitan areas to boot, and second, that every group must be maintained, insofar as it is in public power to maintain it, through an educational system that supports its language and its culture. That, it strikes me, is a recipe for conflict. We will have to do better, and one way of doing so is to explore whether the much maligned goal of assimilation does not still have much to teach us.

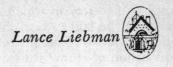

6

Ethnic Groups
and the Legal System

Three stories of the 1970s show the present state of the relationship between law and politics. The stories encourage speculation about: (1) whether the courts are doing something new when they become involved in group conflicts; (2) whether, if new, these involvements are bad; and (3) whether society has alternatives to legal recognition of collective interests and activist legal participation in managing group relations.

A group of black parents in Atlanta filed suit against the local school board in 1958, seeking desegregation. For various reasons, the suit was still in litigation in 1973, by which time two things had happened: other desegregation cases had made clear that Atlanta parents could achieve a broad busing remedy by which more than a hundred years of racially separate schools would finally be altered, and demographic changes had occurred, especially white migration to the Atlanta suburbs and black migration into the city of Atlanta, with the result that the Atlanta school population was more than 80 percent black. In that situation the black parent plaintiffs, organized by the local chapter of the National Association for the Advancement of Colored People (NAACP), decided that an Atlanta busing plan would not serve their interests. This group negotiated a settlement with the school board under which the lawsuit was dropped in return for the board's promise to make a variety of changes in school policies including appointment of black educators to various leadership jobs in the school system. The national NAACP cried foul, saying that the agreement—with its implied denigration of busing—was a bad outcome for blacks nationally, even if correct for the Atlanta circumstances. The national NAACP tried to persuade the federal judge with jurisdiction over the case to reject the settlement. But the judge certified the negotiated agreement, which was affirmed by the U.S. Court of Appeals for the Fifth Circuit.

Parents of retarded youths living at Massachusetts institutions sued the state department of mental health in federal court, alleging that conditions in the institutions deprived their children of their constitutional rights. Facing a long trial, Governor Francis Sargent and his secretary of human services decided that improvement in conditions was a goal they shared and entered negotiations. An agreement was reached, a consent decree signed "settling" the federal lawsuit, and a court monitor appointed. The result has been divided control over the institutions, with many specific matters of policy and program referred to the judge by the monitor. The judge held that the state is required to provide the funds that he believes are required for adequate compliance with the consent decree. Funding has generated controversy in a period of general budget-cutting, and on one occasion the judge threatened the chairmen of the state house and senate ways and means committees with a contempt of court proceeding if their committees did not approve a budget containing the judge's view of necessary funding. Yet no court has ever decided what are the constitutional rights of retarded children, and indeed recent cases from other states suggest that had the Massachusetts case been fully litigated, it is unlikely the children would have received the gains the state promised them in the consent agreement.

Present members of the Passamaquoddy Indian Tribe in Maine sued the U.S. secretary of the interior, alleging that the U.S. was obliged to assert a claim on their behalf to about two-thirds of the land in the state of Maine, because land sales by the ancestors of the Indians in the nineteenth century had been in violation of the federal Nonintercourse Act of 1791, an enactment that barred white men from purchasing Indian land without U.S. government permission. Current landowners (rather, those who thought they owned land until they learned of this lawsuit—

individuals, the state government, local governments, and big timber companies) would have had many possible defenses if the Indians' land claims had ever come to trial: that long-standing nonenforcement of the nonintercourse act rendered it inapplicable; that in any event too much time passed for the claim to be asserted now; that any wrong that did occur 150 and more years ago was a violation as to Indians then alive (whose rights were assertedly violated when they were *allowed* to sell their land for something they preferred at the time), but not a violation that should give rights to persons alive now whose only connection to those mistreated long ago is to be a member of a continuing tribe. Yet even though the likelihood of current Indians recovering large parts of Maine seemed unlikely, the existence of the lawsuit, and certain procedural judgments rendered by a federal judge on preliminary issues, cast such a cloud on title as to be a major deterrent to real estate activity. After six years of citizen anxiety and political posturing, a retired Georgia judge appointed as mediator by President Carter achieved a negotiated agreement by which present members of the tribe are to receive money and some undeveloped land—the money for the Indian plaintiffs and the cash compensation to those giving up land coming from the U.S. Treasury. Ahead lie disputes over who is now eligible to share in the tribe's recovery and how decisions about investing the tribe's new capital should be made.

Today's lawsuits involve the judiciary in a wide range of social issues. Whether the subject is busing or school prayers or abortion or offshore oil drilling or "reverse discrimination," courts are at the center of political and social developments. The explanation for this judicial role is rooted firmly in our history: this is a country that has taken the path of a written constitution, yet a constitution written in "open" phrases that are then committed to judicial interpretation. As of 1803, when John Marshall asserted in *Marbury vs. Madison* that the Supreme Court was to be arbiter of constitutionality when relevant to a litigated matter, the place of the courts in our system of checks and balances has been important. We may never resolve the incompatibility between democratic theory and this role for unelected judges in continually recasting the society's charter, but reopening *Marbury vs. Madison* at this stage in our history seems inconceivable. Indeed, perhaps a country so large and diverse, so lacking in common values, so short of unifying nongovernmental institutions as ours must have some way to determine its basic premises and assert its unifying commitments, and it is this task we have entrusted to the courts.

Because we have assigned to judges the task of protecting and applying our constitutional values, our expectations for their work are very high. We expect them to be different from executive and legislative branches. We think they should be less political and more objective, somehow above the fray. We understand the place of interest groups in politics, but the thought of their intrusion into the judicial sphere seems untenable.

Groups as Plaintiffs and Defendants

Our legal system is founded on an ideology of individualism. The Constitution speaks of "persons" and "citizens." Even the vast business collectivities—the biggest corporations—take their legal identity as a fictional person. The Constitution recognizes states (though not as entities with legal significance predating the Constitution itself), but it and later history refused federal status to municipalities, counties, neighborhoods, and regions, much less to professional societies, economic interest groups, social movements, unions, or families. Invented in the Enlightenment, reared at the height of British empiricism, positivism, and utilitarianism, our legal system is not, or at least was not, at all corporativist, fascist, or collectivist. Our image of law is always of an individual plaintiff and an individual defendant, of equality before the law, of individual rights and responsibilities, of freedom from the sins of one's fathers, of no liability without proof, of individual obligation or responsibility.

Professor Paul Brest of Stanford Law School has written:

> If a society can be said to have an underlying political theory, ours has not been a theory of organic groups but of liberalism, focusing on the rights of individuals, including rights of distributive justice. Of course, we recognize the sociological fact that people desire to affiliate and associate with others who share common interests or characteristics. . . . We grant rights to associations or treat them as fictitious persons only to protect the rights of their individual members. . . . Most societies in which power is formally allocated among racial and national groups are strikingly oppressive, unequal, and unstable.

Yet modern circumstances challenge the reality of that individualist image. Two facts challenge it in particular. First, laws work by creating groups and by assigning consequences to being placed in particular groups. Laws apply to categories of events and to classes of people. They make one rule for optometrists and another for oculists, one subsidy for raspberry growers and another for the artichoke industry, one outcome for those who score seventy-five on a civil service exam and another for those who score seventy-four, one tax rate for the city and another for the suburb, a military draft for those who are twenty-five but not for those who are twenty-six, and so on. As perhaps it is the nature of human thought, it is the nature of law to proceed by presumptions, assumptions, inferences, and generalizations. These group people. And that makes inevitable the question (not the answer) of which groupings are wise/permitted/appropriate and which are not.

Second, groups come to law. Law makes groups, but it also responds to groups. As legislatures are lobbied by groups of constituents who find it efficient to proceed collectively (whether their goal is public housing, nuclear power, sex education, or Ukrainian independence), so opportunities arise to advance common interests by lawsuit, and every sort of economic, geographic, and social group sues and is heard. Assessing this phenomenon, Professor Abram Chayes of Harvard Law School has written: "Perhaps the dominating characteristic of modern federal litigation is that lawsuits do not arise out of disputes between private parties about private rights. Instead, the object of litigation is the vindication of constitutional or statutory policies." Chayes called this new model "public law litigation." Observing it, we may well be tempted to say that the idea of a legal system oriented to individual rights and individual disputes is charming but naive, and that the only prudent intellectual course is to study a legal system now inevitably altered toward a concern for groups and to concentrate our energies on understanding and civilizing that system.

Because the ideology of this society is so clearly oriented toward individualism, the cases summarized at the beginning of this chapter seem strange to us. The courts in each case seem to be acting in an "unjudicial" manner. The questions that must be asked are whether there is something new and important about these instances of legal controversy, whether the courts are really overstepping their bounds, or whether there is some substantive aspect of these cases or of contemporary circumstances that alters the role that the courts must play.

In this light, the interaction between America's legal system and its ethnic groups has been important. Controversies over immigration quotas, access to education and jobs, and arrangements for political representation have required judicial interpretations of the Constitution and of statutes. This much is generally clear and understood. Yet just as important and far less widely perceived is the significance of ethnic developments and controversies for our legal system. Civil rights, desegregation, reapportionment, due process, freedom of speech, dissent and protest, entitlements to minimal income, death penalty, and exclusionary zoning are ethnic issues, frequently fought over in court, that have provided much of the substance for the legal/procedural transformations of the recent past. Our task is to understand how the law, confronted with the sorts of issues that ethnic disputes have brought to it in recent years, has changed its nature and role in society, and, particularly, how this change will affect the country's ethnic groups in the future.

After all, it is not our expectations alone that render the judiciary the peculiar branch that it is. The three cases noted give rise to some difficult questions and not just ones regarding legal procedures. We are troubled when we see group political contention taking place in court, and troubled for good reason. It is one thing for interest groups to enter the legal process. But is the law playing a role in fragmenting the population and then crystallizing that fragmentation? Is it, by giving legal significance to groups, ethnic or otherwise, giving them a stability that may ultimately be harmful to our political system? If we give rights to an Indian tribe or to black parents or even to retarded children, do we make official groups of what might otherwise be— and should be—temporary and shifting alignments? Do we thereby force citizens to classify themselves?

STANDING TO SUE

Every legal regime must have conventions for deciding who can assert interests. In the Anglo-American framework we summarize these conventions with the label "standing." If you are run down on your bicycle by a speeding auto driver, you can sue for damages. Perhaps your spouse can sue for the economic (and other? loss of consortium?) consequences of the accident. If you are killed, perhaps your executor or heirs can sue. Perhaps (recent cases show the endless fertility of standing possibilities) a parent or child who is a bystander can sue, alleging the emotional consequences of witnessing the accident. An unmarried roommate might be able to assert standing, saying the consequences to him or her are much like the effects on a husband or wife.

By definition, standing is the device used to assure that only those parties with a sufficient stake in the outcome of a controversy will be able to obtain judicial resolution of that controversy. In order to have standing to sue, a plaintiff must have a legal right that is being invaded; the party must be "aggrieved" (adversely affected as a result of some statute or other governmental action). Furthermore, standing will only be conferred if there is actual injury in fact to the plaintiffs; there must be a direct causal relationship between action and injury. Generalized concern or "mere interest" in a problem will not be a sufficient basis for standing. Thus, in *Sierra Club vs. Morton*, standing to sue for the preservation of the integrity of a forest was denied because the plaintiff organization failed to assert facts showing that it was directly affected by the action. Standing, therefore, is the ability of a party to assert that his or her own legal right was invaded and that he or she has in fact been injured by the action taken.

So much is easy and routine. Though the law of standing may change with our perception of legally relevant impacts and interests, it has remained based upon our understanding of the society as one composed of autonomous individuals; the person with standing is the person who has been harmed or whose rights have been infringed; the harm or infringement is more or less directly traceable from defendant to plaintiff; the lawsuit has a traditional format of one on one.

With the rising importance of groups in the legal system, the application of the concept of standing has had to change. This is the consequence of the new sense of group political relationships bounded and certified by legal (and legally enforceable) rights and obligations. Consider: if Maine's Indians or Atlanta's black parents or Massachusetts's retarded children have legal rights that government has failed to satisfy, then they must have standing to sue. And indeed, in a large number of cases, courts have accorded standing to groups that have alleged a sufficiently direct "injury-in-fact," thus validating the existence of these groups as legal entities with legal rights.

United States vs. Students Challenging Regulatory Agency Procedures (SCRAP), for example, was an action by an unincorporated association against an increase in freight rates that might have had undesirable effects on the environment. Because SCRAP asserted that its members used the environment for activities that had suffered as a result of the rate changes, the court found that there was alleged a direct injury-in-fact traceable to the increase in rates and granted standing.

GROUP RIGHTS

Standing, however, is but the procedural expression of an important issue. Central is the notion of rights that do not inhere in an individual. There are rights against a punch in the nose and against trespass upon one's land and to receive 100 bales of hay for which one had contracted. No one has quantified, but it seems correct to assume that 50 or 100 years ago these were the bulk of the social and economic relationships regulated by law. Government had its sovereign functions and its role as administrator and enforcer of private decisions and agreements. Now, so many of the important transactions involve government as a more active participant. Almost inevitably, because government is big and can function only by classifying and because citizens and firms can only influence government by banding together, group relationships take center stage, shoving individual transactions to the wings.

Legal rights take on a different dimension when they are being asserted by groups rather than by individuals. Is there a right to be educated in an integrated school? No, but there is a right not to be a member of a group victimized by political acts motivated by a segregatory purpose, a right "remedied" (to a degree) by a rearrangement of school districts. Or there may be a "right" that one's school district not suffer from state taxing and spending rules that leave some districts with large resources and few students and other districts with many students and a small tax base. The remedy may be a revised tax system, but it will by no means assure a certain level of school spending, much less a certain sort or quantum of education. Is there a "right" to a pension? Perhaps not, only a right to have a large fund invested carefully, for the benefit of all retirees, and to have rules of distribution meet a judge's standard of fairness and relevance. Education, zoning, taxation, job opportunities, pensions—by their nature, these social goods exist in relationship to and as a member of groups.

When government becomes a major actor concerning land use and job distribution and benefits, its involvement—whether it is regulating or distributing or taking—must meet the standards of due process, and so the rights to these benefits become to a degree "legalized." We thus begin to use the language of "rights." But as to this sort of social claim, the "right" is collective or relative or contingent or procedural. The claim itself has much of its meaning in status, in relative position. With these claims, therefore, the questions of which group one is in, with whom one is classified, and where different groups stand with regard to one another become absolutely central. Some legal claims always had these characteristics. But there has been a change in degree—an increase in the significance of assertions of these sorts that has by now probably become a change in kind.

Of course the questions about standing and about rights, which are really questions about how attenuated the effect of unlawful action can be on the person who brings a lawsuit, are trickier than those that arise in the traditional litigation. The victim, the person punched or the person trespassed upon or the person who did not receive the hay, could sue. But who is the victim of racial segregation in housing, and who is in the group that has a legal right to sue to stop it? In a case now pending in the U.S. Supreme Court, the Court will decide whether a lawsuit can be brought by a "tester"—a person hired by a private antidiscrimination organization in Richmond, Virginia, to visit real estate brokers in order to document racial "steering" to neighborhoods. If discrimination is an offense only against the black family who genuinely wants an apartment and is falsely told there are no vacancies in a white building or subdivision, then the "tester" would not have "standing" to sue because he or she would only be claiming that someone else's rights have been invaded rather than asserting that his or her own rights were directly injured. But if nondiscrimination is a right of all who care, because integration is a value protected for all, then those concerned about the racial composition of neighborhoods should be able to sue, even if they are not themselves looking to buy a house. Or perhaps an out-of-neighborhood tester would not have standing but someone residing in the neighborhood would. Is preservation of a mountain the right only of the person who hikes on it or also of one who hopes to hike on it someday or who looks at photographs of it with extra pleasure because it is still there or who only knows in general that mountains are being protected? Because we have ordered society in new ways, granting "rights" much subtler and more diffuse than the traditional assurances against concrete and personal injury; because, it can be said, we have enough to eat and can indulge more sophisticated claims; and because technology connects us to distant consequences and science lets us see new causal relationships (think of a "right" that aerosol sprays not destroy the ozone layer in ways tragic for our grandchildren), we confront these questions of standing, which alter the nature of the lawsuit.

REPRESENTATION

In a group context, the ability to sue raises more questions than the subtle relationship between the right and the harm. Because the "party" involved, plaintiff or defendant, is not an individual but a group of individuals, there may be disagreement within the single party over how the legal claim should be managed, what the real issue is, and who should be chosen to argue the case. In the school busing example, who picked the Atlanta NAACP, or the national NAACP, to represent the black parents? How do we know that parents prefer an associate superintendent's job to busing? Dean Derrick Bell of the University of Oregon Law School has written incisively of the power that inevitably flows to interest-group lawyers—whether working for the Legal Defense Fund, the Sierra Club, Ralph Nader, or, indeed, the U.S. Department of Justice. Their sense of the possibilities, their knowledge of the system, means that their values play a large role, especially since the members of the client organizations get most of their knowledge from the lawyers and since individuals among the client groups rarely have enough at stake to become sufficiently knowledgeable to play a major role.

But the issue is more complicated than merely a matter of relations between group members and lawyers or the inevitably chaotic arrangements for selection of leaders and internal decision-making in a private organization. We are now recognizing that important matters are being decided by "political" lawsuits, in which nongovernmental groups are litigants: parties plaintiff and parties defendant. Those groups—environmental groups, fair-housing groups, neighborhood associations, ethnic associations—have neither the regular and governmentally regulated structure of the corporation nor the single focus on profit of the corporation and the partnership. Legislative decision-making long ago made such groupings (known there as lobbies, pressure groups, interest groups) important. But the legislative process contains mechanisms for screening and weighing group representations and is suited to an endless overlap and flux of groups as the agenda of issues changes. By contrast, the traditional lawsuit is a single formal event. It takes place by procedures premised on the model of the search for truth about a single past event, that truth to be determined after adversary participation by two parties whose interests are opposed. Now we have lawsuits vastly more like legislative proceedings: they have many parties, arranged in shifting alliances; they go on for a long time; they look to the future instead of resolving a matter from the past; they often seek "equity" or "balance" or "fairness" instead of determining which of two opposed contentions is correct; the result is sometimes a compromise among values that cannot all be achieved and the creation of procedures for living together in the future.

Lawmaking in elected legislatures, while presenting ancient and serious questions of representation, conflict-of-interest, resolution-of-differences, and unfairness to permanent minorities, is a satisfactory means of making official decisions drawing upon the preferences of a diverse and diversely organized citizenry. With the lawsuit as a process for making a subset of those decisions (decisions about the distribution of income, about control over public services, about institutional rules for making other ongoing decisions), we must face the problem of the formal legitimation of parties at law, instead of the mere inducement to groups to seek a voice in the legislature.

When the doctrine of standing announces finally who has an adequate "interest" to sue, it certifies the group's membership and goals and procedures for making decisions. The legal process holds the group together, at least for purposes of sharing in legal winnings and being responsible for legal liabilities.

The problem that this raises is made very clear in the ethnic context. We hear often that "blacks" or "Italians" or "Mormons" or "Catholics" have a view about legislation: for busing, against abortion, for school prayers, against the MX missile, for stricter enforcement of immigration rules. We know that the statements we read are only more or less accurate, that representatives express what they want as a group's view, that some members of the broad group may be fervently opposed to the supposed group position, and that indeed the position may have the support (much less the attention and enthusiasm) of group members to a wide extent, but may well not. It is altogether different when "the Passamaquoddy Tribe," or "a class consisting of all nonwhite children in Atlanta" or "parents of all retarded children in Massachusetts" are plaintiffs in a lawsuit and so only one voice is being heard as representative of the group's goals. Yet we should not rush to the conclusion that the courts are the wrong place to resolve group disputes.

Is it inevitable, or even happy, that urban politics is so often an ethnic battleground? Isn't it the case that has been true in our cities since the earliest waves of immigration? Haven't we always had ethnic disputes over jobs, turf, and schools? Is it important that the forum for these disputes now is often the courtroom? Isn't that just a sign that we have taken steps toward codifying aspects of social life, and that modern explicitness about officially valid claims imports the courts as interpreters and regulators of processes of government allocation?

To avoid the courts' entrance into a realm traditionally unassociated with judicial activity, shouldn't other parts of government do more and better? After all, courts rarely seize power; they fill gaps left by the inadequate work of other institutions. For example, when Congress enacts laws, can it draft with less ambiguity, controlling its tendency to appear to stand on both sides of difficult choices? (As just one instance, consider the *Lau* case discussed by Professor Cafferty in chapter 4, in which Congress did not say whether it was or was not creating a right to bilingual education.) Can other mechanisms of dispute resolution —everything from school disciplinary hearings to teacher–school board collective bargaining—resolve disputes without their reaching the courts?

But the real question is whether a larger degree of agreement

can be reached about the boundaries of rights. While public
sector services and tasks were expanding after 1960, but also
more recently as retrenchments have occurred, we have made
very little progress toward agreed assumptions about minimal
entitlements or citizen responsibilities or appropriate shares. By
certain measures, our welfare state arrangements are now comparable to those in Europe. But we have nothing like the European *theory*—the agreement as to what a citizen can expect.
Without theory and explanation, we have to proceed chaotically,
with every public service and every public decision being a
matter to be fought over. Given the different levels of government that result from federalism and the unrestricted range of
claims that can be asserted, it has to occur that ambiguity and
overlap make courts the agency of reconciliation and minimal
coherence. Unless we clarify our promises and understandings,
we must continue to battle in court.

The law will continue to muddle through the procedural
difficulties that result from group social controversies. All the
complexity of standing and representation and remedy only reflects difficulty in defining rights. It is hard for a society to decide
what retarded children are entitled to, whether Indians (or
Japanese-Americans interred during World War II) should be
compensated today because of what now looks like mistreatment
of their ancestors, what rights should result from proven illegal
school desegregation. But it is not unworthy when a society tries
to decide them. Given our traditions, lawsuits will be a significant
part of the decision process. If the cases are not traditional—if
the judges become managers of ongoing group disputes with very
little stable law to guide them—then the courts might do less
good work than they do in conventional lawsuits. But the question that will remain is whether we can proceed institutionally
in ways that would make these imperfect judicial efforts unnecessary.

If the lawsuit is a branch of politics, then our concerns about
ethnic explicitness in the courtrooms should be similar to the
concerns we have when ethnicity is at the center of legislative and
electoral battles. If ethnicity is important to individuals, then
they will formulate claims against society in ethnic terms. They
will form groups, select leaders, find money, and generally fight
to seek or to defend what is important to them. In legislative and

administrative processes and in the hurly-burly of electoral contests, this is normal and traditional. Now it is becoming normal and traditional in court as well, because the court is the forum for part of the action. When the court hears the case, it confers legitimacy on the association or organization or merely on the unorganized collection of people with a similar interest around whom the lawyers have thrown their net. This makes for disorderly lawsuits, for internal disputes among groups of litigants, and for new doctrinal complexities about who is later barred because someone claiming to speak for them has had a day in court. By itself, however, it is only a problem in judicial management, not a threat to society. The asserted threat arises when legal outcomes—whether statutes or court decisions—grant rights according to ethnic or racial classifications. That is the issue now posed at the forefront of equal protection analysis, and it is discussed in the next section.

Equal Protection of the Laws

The law's relationship to groups of citizens has received its most interesting and important development in the context of judicial interpretation of the equal protection clause, an ambiguous section of the Fourteenth Amendment with open-ended wording and history that are surely an invitation to and a sanction for an active judicial role of interpretation and enforcement.

What is "equal protection of the laws"? The law cannot be equal to the person who steals and the person who does not, the person who scores higher on a civil service test and the person who scores lower, the person whose taxes are levied on an income of $10,000 and the person who reports income of $300,000. Laws classify and distinguish. Thus the constitutional question must be which classifications, which distinctions, are constitutionally acceptable.

It asks the same question, in a harder form, to inquire which groups the law can create. One possible interpretation of the equal protection clause, for example, is as a denunciation of classifications according to race. Perhaps the draftsmen and ratifiers in 1868 meant to bar laws disadvantaging blacks by placing them in legally disfavored categories. And, indeed, for the first seventy-five years of the amendment's life, it was interpreted to strike

down legal disabilities imposed on blacks ("No Negro may . . ."),
but not racial separation mandated by legislation (separate
schools, separate army units, bars to miscegenation, and so forth).

When, with *Brown vs. Board of Education* the signal moment,
the Fourteenth Amendment was made the principal weapon in
the assault on legally mandated segregation, we invited into our
discourse not only the many hard questions of sociology and
morality and politics, but also quite difficult questions of constitutional jurisprudence, whose contours could only be dimly
glimpsed by the judges who began the process. Now, moving
into the second quarter century since the *Brown* case, we can
appraise the idea of equal protection as it currently looks, keeping in mind Archibald Cox's pithy comment, "Once loosed, the
idea of equality is not easily cabined."

OTHER GROUPS

The Fourteenth Amendment does not speak of blacks. It thus
seems to establish an ideal of equal treatment that is relevant to
the entire population. Yet, as stated above, laws must discrim-
inate; that is their nature. Thus we must ask which discriminations, which inequalities, are forbidden by the Constitution.
Considering everything that we know about the circumstances
of 1868, it must be the case that discriminations against blacks
on account of their race were the chief purpose the amendment's
draftsmen had in mind. Certainly nothing in the intervening
years makes that purpose any less essential to a constitutional
regime today.

But why do we want our Constitution to bar, and our judges
to prohibit, discriminations on account of skin color? Because
the country practiced, and the Constitution explicitly sanctioned,
slavery; because we believe racial discrimination to be an especially prevalent and dangerous tendency of mankind, needing the
most serious institutional barriers that we can structure; because
we know that a great deal of racial hostility exists today, render-
ing unacceptable government actions and decisions that are not
justified. We fear that without a constitutional barrier to discrimination, government decisions would classify blacks to their
detriment, either because of bigotry or because of decisions to
treat blacks separately that are efficient but that we have committed ourselves to forbid.

Concentrating on these commitments, it is inevitable that we see the possibility that the same arguments are available as to other groups in society. Should we not subject to judicial scrutiny legislative and administrative decisions that grant different legal statuses not to whites and blacks but to other groups within the population?

For this chapter, it is inappropriate to write at length about sex discrimination and the Fourteenth Amendment. The law classified extensively between males and females at the time the Fourteenth Amendment was adopted. Longstanding interpretations accepted these classifications. The most famous quotation is from Justice Bradley's opinion in *Bradwell vs. Illinois*, the 1873 case which upheld the state's refusal to let a woman practice law:

> The natural and proper timidity and delicacy which belongs to the female sex evidently unfits it for many of the occupations of civil life. The constitution of the family organization, which is founded in the divine ordinance, as well as in the nature of things, indicates the domestic sphere as that which properly belongs to the domain and functions of womanhood. . . . The paramount destiny and mission of woman are to fulfill the noble and benign offices of wife and mother. This is the law of the Creator.

One approach to that state of the law is a constitutional amendment. And indeed Congress approved the Equal Rights Amendment, but it now appears that even with an extended period for ratification the requisite thirty-eight states will not approve the Equal Rights Amendment.

Nevertheless, Supreme Court interpretations of the Fourteenth Amendment have moved a substantial distance from *Bradwell* and have invalidated a range of government actions classifying by sex. They have, indeed, suggested an active judicial role in assuring that government actions not be based on "old notions" or "assumptions of dependency" or "the role typing society has long imposed" or "the traditional way of thinking about females." Most recently, however, in the June 1981 opinion upholding males-only draft registration, the Court has turned the other way (though it is easy to imagine a judiciary that struck down much that reflected traditional ideas about sex roles but was not willing to be the institution of government that took even the tiniest step toward sending women into military combat).

It is important to observe the differences from issues concerning racial distinctions. Women are a group not legally barred from political power, not weak because they are oppressed by others, but weak only when women themselves choose not to assert their own claims. Yet history and culture and former legal arrangements play a role in keeping many women from pressing what some women and some men think is their true right and interest. Do judges have the task of "correcting" for those impacts of culture? If so, their mandate comes only from the words "equal protection of the laws," a thin support indeed, linguistically and historically. But is it imaginable, in a society in which women's roles are changing, that courts will decline to be one institutional agent of a movement so widely accepted in the circles in which judges travel? Yet does not an active judicial role concerning sexual stereotyping, at a time of judicial hesitation concerning, for example, economic rights, emphasize the charge of elitism and hostility to true democracy so often leveled at judicial review?

For purposes of this chapter, there is a far more important group that has sometimes been accorded status as a sector protected against hostile legislation. The group is aliens. Aliens normally have no voice or vote in politics. Laws, enacted by citizens, often classify aliens unfavorably. In a series of cases concerning eligibility for jobs, the Supreme Court has sometimes required that these laws be supported by a public purpose that is "substantial" and "necessary," but in other cases has asked only for "some rational relationship" between the classification and a public purpose. For example, they allow state government to deny aliens jobs as state policemen (Justice Stevens, dissenting, said the law would deny the New York State Police the services of Hercule Poirot or Sherlock Holmes) and as school teachers but bar the state from preventing their certification as lawyers. But the issue is immensely important, given the large legal and illegal alien population.

Most of the arguments for judicial protection of blacks apply to aliens. One argument, however, is stronger: aliens have no participation in politics, and so have far less opportunity than blacks to advance their interests without resort to the courts. Otherwise, they are a distinguishable group, are often the subject of prejudice, and have difficulty escaping this status to meld into the larger population. Unlike blacks, aliens were not slaves. But a powerful argument can be made that tolerable, not to say decent or defensible, domestic relations in a country with millions of aliens requires active scrutiny of the majority's laws concerning those aliens whom it chooses or permits to enter. Otherwise, the country will contain a substantial population without access to *any* branch of government, a class likely to become entrenched in cycles of inferior position. If the nation is not to repeat its history as slaveholder and is not to make all the mistakes of Europe's foreign-worker history, it cannot exclude aliens from all institutional redress.

The issue is presented squarely in the lawsuits asking whether the states are constitutionally required to provide public education for the children of unlawful immigrants. Other cases will follow. For example:

1. Must government (or perhaps a private firm) keep its promises to aliens? For example, what of the promises implicitly made when a worker pays the social security tax?
2. Are unequal work conditions constitutional? What of a lesser minimum wage for alien workers, for example? Or reduced Occupational Safety and Health Administration (OSHA) protection for aliens?
3. Is there a minimal set of "citizenship" rights (speech? due process? freedom from unreasonable search?) that is an attribute of humanity, not deniable to any human being who is within the country?
4. It is worth noting that aliens are particularly in need of the group access to the courts discussed above. How will they come to have representation? Will we, for example, permit Mexico to represent its citizens who are temporarily in this country?

Focusing on noncitizen residents, lawful or unlawful, as a group at least arguably appropriate for the special judicial protection that the Fourteenth Amendment certainly grants to blacks and may grant to women opens up the even harder question concerning persons of Hispanic origin. Along a continuum, this categorization is a short distance from aliens. Many, of course, *are* aliens. The group as a whole faces major barriers in participating politically. Prejudice is substantial. Language is a major barrier. How can one imagine a Constitution that protects black Americans and does not speak to the circumstances, similar in so many ways, of Americans who are recently from Puerto Rico or Mexico or, indeed, Cuba or Haiti?

On the other hand, that is the problem: if blacks mean Puerto Ricans which mean Haitians, how can one stop before Latvians or Japanese or Italians or Scots? But there is an answer. Recall that we are considering here judicial scrutiny of laws which themselves classify in certain ways. Laws disadvantaging blacks have almost uniformly been struck down. Laws disadvantaging and advantaging women are now the subject of extensive litigation. Laws about aliens are frequently litigated. Where there are laws classifying citizens of Hispanic origin, surely they should survive only if their necessity and appropriateness and fairness are reviewed and validated by a court.

And there are such laws, in the form of laws which make the English language this country's official tongue. The hard and immediate question is whether the Constitution should protect citizens (also aliens?) whose English is limited or nonexistent by intrusive judicial review of legislative arrangements that insist upon the priority of English. Sixty years ago, pluralists praised Supreme Court decisions that protected the rights of parents to educate their children in German. How far does the Constitution permit the majority to go in insisting that public business be done in English, and in encouraging all persons to adapt to an English-language country, if the effect is frequent inconvenience, and sometimes real hardship, for those who were reared in other tongues? The question is difficult. But it is impossible to deny that it is a *constitutional* question, appropriate in our system for judicial consideration.

When one begins to list the groups on whose behalf courts have reviewed legislation—blacks, women, aliens, Mexican-Americans —one quickly sees that the list is potentially very large. Are we to accord judicial review to the claim of any group whom society has treated badly? Then why not provide judicial protection for bank robbers! Is our standard "groups that can't win battles for themselves in the legislature"? Then every law about which someone complains creates a candidate, because in every instance the legislative decision has been adverse to a group that is, therefore, now aggrieved. Is our standard "groups whom the legislature treats worse than it should"? Then who is to say whether the legislature was right? We can mention the physically handicapped, drug addicts, prisoners, homosexuals, the elderly, and even retarded children. The arguments are subtly different in each case. For now, it is only important to say that we have created the potential for very wide judicial involvement in basic and controversial domestic politics, and that we do not yet have a limiting principle that tells why any group other than blacks can successfully request intrusive judicial review when the legislature has acted to their detriment, yet confines the principle so that it stops any place short of the groups referred to above. That problem remains very serious for this society.

DISCRIMINATORY IMPACT OR DISCRIMINATORY MOTIVATION

One way the law has recently grappled with the asserted rights of groups has been in deciding which distinctions require strict judicial scrutiny under the equal protection clause—deciding, in effect, the length of the list of suspicious categorizations, a list that begins with categorizations disadvantaging minority races. The second way the issue of groups has arisen under the equal protection clause has been in judicial review of the *impact,* as opposed to the *motivation,* of government action.

Start with the easy case: the constitutional certainty that in 1982 the legislature cannot deny the vote to blacks or the practice of law to women or driver's licenses to persons who cannot speak English. Government cannot draw lines it cannot justify, and in each of these cases the courts will look hard at the justification to see if it fits closely with some legitimate public goal. No fit has been found close enough to justify a law disadvantaging blacks.

Now comes a more complex case: just as the legislature cannot say it is making a category of blacks and treating that category worse (and, in many contexts, cannot do so as to women or aliens or some of the other groups discussed above), so it cannot make a decision that on its face does not mention blacks but is *in fact* motivated by an attempt to disadvantage blacks. If it can be shown that a zoning change was denied because the zoning board did not want moderate-income housing that would attract blacks or if a school district was altered to prevent racial integration, the government actions are unconstitutional, even though on their face they appear neutral and conventional. Of course, it is hard to prove motivation, especially in a chaotic legislative process, and, of course, difficult doctrinal questions arise when an official action obviously stems from a number of purposes, some of them valid and one invalid, but the general principle is clear.

Now comes the third type of case: government makes a decision that does not mention blacks. It reduces public housing subsidies or rezones a city's schools or closes a swimming pool. No antiblack motivation is shown; indeed, there is an entirely legitimate explanation for the decision, for instance, budget-balancing. But the result of the decision—its impact, as opposed to its motivation—is harmful to blacks (or, as the case may be, women or Puerto Ricans or Japanese-Americans or homosexuals).

For a time ten years ago, it appeared the Supreme Court was about to interpret the equal protection clause to forbid such decisions, or at least to require that government canvass alternative ways to achieve its legitimate purposes before acting in such a way. That direction in constitutional doctrine could be fairly clearly sketched at the very end of the tenure of the Warren Court. It was, however, swiftly rejected after President Nixon's appointees took their seats, and it is now commonplace that no constitutional violation can be established solely with proof of the racially disparate results of government action.

The idea lives, however, both because certain commentators continue to urge it, and more importantly because statutes have been interpreted as creating something quite like it with respect to important areas of social life. In particular, Title VII of the 1964 Civil Rights Act, the provision barring discrimination in employment, has been held to mean that unless an employer can show a close connection between a job criterion and the requirements of a job, it cannot use the criterion (for example, a standardized "intelligence" test or a requirement of a high school diploma) if it has a differential impact on black applicants, even if the company established the criterion in good faith. Also, the Voting Rights Act of 1965 bars portions of the country from changing their local election systems, for instance, their districts, if the change diminishes black representation, even if the change was not motivated by racism. Thus, we have major and continuing experience with the idea of making sure that satisfactorily motivated decisions (whom to hire, how to structure local government) do not have a result that is bad for blacks as a group, at least not without a compelling justification. We have also had extensive experience with a "group-disadvantage" principle in what are essentially remedial contexts: as when, after a finding of so-called de jure segregation (by a school board or an employer, for instance), a court orders correction of the present consequences of the former misdeeds, and, in a different sort of remedial context, when the court orders payments of cash and land to Indian groups, to Alaskan natives, and, as is now being discussed, to Japanese-Americans who were forcibly interred during World War II. (Nearly fifteen years ago, Professor Boris Bittker of the Yale Law School explored in depth the issue of cash compensation for slavery and segregation in his book *The Case for Black Reparations.*)

The questions that are put by these developments are difficult and important. Are we prepared to trust the political process, as it reaches outcomes that affect blacks and whites differently? Can blacks do well enough politically so that we regard the outcomes —even if sometimes difficult for them—as compatible with our ideals of a just society? If they can, then the courts should not evaluate "consequences," should not be concerned with the "discriminatory impact" of political decisions. If, on the other hand, an obligation still exists because of slavery and legally-mandated segregation, if racism is prevalent and offensive, if politics remains contaminated as it acts differently upon blacks and whites, if blacks still need and deserve help as they struggle for full membership in this society, if there is a great deal of political action that we believe is motivated by antiblack animus but we have trouble proving that in particular cases, and if (a very big if) a fair shake for blacks can be achieved through judicial supervision of political outcomes without that process having unacceptable consequences for our ultimate goals of equality and justice, *then* courts should invalidate under the equal protection clause legislative and administrative decisions that have a differential and negative impact on blacks and which cannot be justified by some adequate showing of necessity or appropriateness. Or, even if we do not wish to apply such review as a constitutional matter to all government decisions, we might regard jobs and voting as so important (and perhaps educational access also) that we should insist that decisions on job criteria and on electoral arrangements either be fair to blacks in their results *or* be shown to be necessary to achieve some legitimate purpose.

That said, it is suddenly right to see the difference between blacks in America and all other classifications of persons: women,

Hispanics, Italians, Vietnamese, handicapped, gays, and so forth. Only with blacks is the social obligation so clear and so strong. And only to blacks (and as to American Indians, where many of the legal issues have a special context that there was not room to discuss in this chapter) is there so much reason to fear that the give and take of politics will have consistently bad outcomes. It is possible to argue, as Professor Glazer has done in chapter 5 and in other distinguished writings, that we should let politics work for all groups including blacks and give legal place only to individuals and not to blacks and others as groups. But it is important to note at least the possibility of continuing for a time to accord legal protection to the concerns of black Americans while acknowledging that legal scrutiny of political and economic outcomes should not extend beyond blacks, should not categorize and Balkanize the entire population, should not repress fluid and inevitable group political maneuvering, should not—except as to blacks—review the justice of political outcomes as they affect officially classified groups of citizens, but only review allegations of discriminatory motivation.

The final issue that requires discussion is affirmative action. If the Constitution tells legislatures they cannot classify blacks to their detriment, can they nonetheless classify minority racial groups to their advantage? This is certainly the most divisive constitutional issue of our day. Its difficulty is reflected in the lack of coherence of the major Supreme Court decisions on the subject; the Court, like the country, finds the questions hard, close, and troubling. At the moment, however, the Court seems to have said that the Constitution does permit Congress to make special provision for blacks, at least in certain circumstances of past discrimination and present inequality and at least where the consequences for disfavored whites are tolerable. And indeed, while it has proved difficult for constitutional scholars and moral philosophers to articulate the explanation, there is certainly a large difference between a legislative attempt to perpetuate a race in an inferior position and efforts to pursue eventual equality by correcting for present consequences of past discrimination. Professor Weaver makes the argument in chapter 3, and his quotation from William Coleman makes it too.

It is also important, however, as Professor Glazer notes, to see the way in which affirmative action efforts tend to legitimize formal categorizations of the population, racial and other, and to transform distributional questions into issues of group share. The reason is not only that the arguments for affirmative protection for blacks have aspects that apply to women, Hispanics, the elderly, and gays. Another, equally important, reason is that subjecting distributional outcomes to justification (as, for instance, when private employers were forced to show a job-related justification for educational criteria or public employers for civil service examinations) has stripped away veils which cannot easily be restored, and that intense scrutiny has been generally delegitimizing. If there is no defensible basis for picking a school principal or a factory foreman and if the social significance of and the economic return to the position are so high, how justify any method except a lottery on the one hand or quotas of race and sex and ethnicity and age on the other?

We will have to struggle with these questions for some time. Meanwhile, perhaps we should hope for a Supreme Court wise enough and ingenious enough to uphold legislative decisions that assist blacks but refuse to uphold, because the justifications are weaker and the costs to the social fabric so great, extensions of those arrangements to other groups. Lincoln said we might suffer for slavery "until every drop of blood drawn with the lash shall be paid." As to all other social groupings, all those who were never enslaved, majority attitudes and policies can change and even progress, but an attempt to assess and correct guilt is the wrong, and indeed an unconstitutional endeavor.

Index

About The American Assembly

The American Assembly was established by Dwight D. Eisenhower at Columbia University in 1950. It holds nonpartisan meetings and publishes authoritative books to illuminate issues of United States policy.

An affiliate of Columbia, with offices in the Graduate School of Business, the Assembly is a national educational institution incorporated in the State of New York.

The Assembly seeks to provide information, stimulate discussion, and evoke independent conclusions in matters of vital public interest.

AMERICAN ASSEMBLY SESSIONS

At least two national programs are initiated each year. Authorities are retained to write background papers presenting essential data and defining the main issues in each subject.

A group of men and women representing a broad range of experience, competence, and American leadership meet for several days to discuss the Assembly topic and consider alternatives for national policy.

All Assemblies follow the same procedure. The background papers are sent to participants in advance of the Assembly. The Assembly meets in small groups for four or five lengthy periods. All groups use the same agenda. At the close of these informal sessions, participants adopt in plenary session a final report of findings and recommendations.

Regional, state, and local Assemblies are held following the national session at Arden House. Assemblies have also been held in England, Switzerland, Malaysia, Canada, the Caribbean, South America, Central America, the Philippines, and Japan. Over one hundred thirty institutions have co-sponsored one or more Assemblies.

ARDEN HOUSE

Home of the American Assembly and scene of the national sessions is Arden House which was given to Columbia University in 1950 by W. Averell Harriman. E. Roland Harriman joined his brother in contributing toward adaptation of the property for conference purposes. The buildings and surrounding land, known as the Harriman Campus of Columbia University, are 50 miles north of New York City.

Arden House is a distinguished conference center. It is self-supporting and operates throughout the year for use by organizations with educational objectives.

The background papers for each Assembly are published in cloth and paperbound editions for use by individuals, libraries, businesses, public agencies, nongovernmental organizations, educational institutions, discussion and service groups. In this way the deliberations of Assembly sessions are continued and extended.

The subjects of Assembly programs to date are:

1951——United States-Western Europe Relationships
1952——Inflation
1953——Economic Security for Americans
1954——The United States' Stake in the United Nations
——The Federal Government Service
1955——United States Agriculture
——The Forty-Eight States
1956——The Representation of the United States Abroad
——The United States and the Far East
1957——International Stability and Progress
——Atoms for Power
1958——The United States and Africa
——United States Monetary Policy
1959——Wages, Prices, Profits, and Productivity
——The United States and Latin America
1960——The Federal Government and Higher Education
——The Secretary of State
——Goals for Americans
1961——Arms Control: Issues for the Public
——Outer Space: Prospects for Man and Society
1962——Automation and Technological Change
——Cultural Affairs and Foreign Relations
1963——The Population Dilemma
——The United States and the Middle East
1964——The United States and Canada
——The Congress and America's Future
1965——The Courts, the Public, and the Law Explosion
——The United States and Japan
1966——State Legislatures in American Politics
——A World of Nuclear Powers?
——The United States and the Philippines
——Challenges to Collective Bargaining
1967——The United States and Eastern Europe
——Ombudsmen for American Government?